# Wagner Rehearsing the 'Ring'

Heinrich Porges

# Wagner Rehearsing the 'Ring'

*An Eye-Witness Account of
the Stage Rehearsals of
the First Bayreuth Festival*

Heinrich Porges

*translated by*

Robert L. Jacobs

Cambridge University Press

*Cambridge*
London   New York   New Rochelle
Melbourne   Sydney

Published by the Press Syndicate of the University of Cambridge
The Pitt Building, Trumpington Street, Cambridge CB2 1RP
32 East 57th Street, New York, NY 10022, USA
296 Beaconsfield Parade, Middle Park, Melbourne 3206, Australia

Originally published in German as *Die Bühnenproben zu den Bayreuther Festspielen des Jahres 1876*, appearing first in instalments in the *Bayreuther Blätter* between 1881 and 1896. Publication in book form:
*Das Rheingold*, Verlag von Ernst Schmeitzner, Chemnitz, 1881
*Die Walküre*, Verlag von Ernst Schmeitzner, Chemnitz, 1882
*Siegfried*, Verlag von Siegismund & Volkening, Leipzig, 1896
*Götterdämmerung*, Verlag von Siegismund & Volkening, Leipzig, 1896

First published in English by Cambridge University Press 1983
as *Wagner Rehearsing the 'Ring': An Eye-Witness Account of the Stage Rehearsals of the First Bayreuth Festival*
© Cambridge University Press 1983

Printed in Great Britain at
the University Press, Cambridge

Library of Congress catalogue card number: 82-12787

British Library Cataloguing in Publication Data
Porges, Heinrich
Wagner rehearsing the 'Ring'.
1. Wagner, Richard. Ring des Nibelungen
2. Opera—Germany (West)—Bayreuth—
Production and direction.
I. Title II. Die Bühnenproben zu den
Bayreuther Festspielen des Jahres 1876. English
782. 1'092'4 ML410. W15

ISBN 0 521 23722 X

# Contents

# Translator's Preface

꧂

A witty producer of operas, noted for his enterprise, recently dismissed his critics with the remark that each wrote 'as though he had a private line to Parnassus'. Such a 'private line' is provided by this authoritative record of what Wagner said and did during the stage rehearsals of the first Bayreuth festival and of how he regarded the *Ring*.

On 6 November 1872 Wagner wrote the following letter to Heinrich Porges:

> I have you in mind for a task which will be of the greatest importance to the future of my enterprise. I want you to follow all my rehearsals very closely ... and to note down everything I say, even the smallest details, about the interpretation and performance of our work, so that a tradition goes down in writing.

The late Curt von Westernhagen, in his recently translated *Wagner: A Biography*, after quoting this letter, paid a glowing tribute to the book which resulted, *Die Bühnenproben zu den Bayreuther Festspielen des Jahres 1876*:

> Porges devoted himself to the task conscientiously and with amazing insight and perception. He was not only thoroughly familiar with the score . . . but also, thanks to his education and culture, fully able to appreciate its literary and philosophical content. We sense the fresh air of first-hand experience in his description of how Wagner transformed himself into each character ... The distinguishing characteristic ... is his ability always to locate the endless detail of Wagner's individual instructions ... in an over-all intellectual context.[1]

We all know that in many respects the actual performances themselves fell short, that Richter's tempos were faulty, that the Siegfried was a disappointment, that only the Alberich (Karl Hill) was outstanding, that scene changes were bungled, that the dragon's neck was missing. In the 'fresh air' of Porges' record we experience Wagner's vision of the ideal, a vision of both the microcosm and the macrocosm. Woglinde's delivery of the Renunciation

1. Cambridge 1978, pp. 489-90.

of Love motive must be utterly impersonal, the melody 'must have the chiselled quality of a piece of sculpture'; the accents must fall upon the upper notes of the Donner motive when it is thundered out in the prelude to the first act of *Die Walküre* ('"Play it with greater awareness!" [Wagner] kept calling') and the staccato of the strings' crotchets as they die away 'should be weighty, not pointed'; the tempo of the Magic Fire music at the close of Wotan's Farewell should be dictated by the need to make each semiquaver of the harps' figure 'clearly perceptible'. And so on and so on, accompanied throughout by music examples – 411 of them – and accompanied by, or rather one should say accompanying, general directives of vital importance. The audibility of the words was 'a problem that constantly cropped up during the rehearsals'. It was not only that when Sieglinde, whom Brünnhilde has rescued, wishes to know who it was that bade Brünnhilde do so ('Wer hiess dich Maid, dem Harst mich entführen?') every word must be clearly articulated, 'otherwise all was lost'; every word of the assembling Valkyries' exchanges must also be audible: 'to ensure this it should be the rule to deliver all passages of dialogue . . . weightily in a restrained tempo and return to the original faster tempo for the elemental, exultant outbursts'. In another context Porges writes: 'Wagner declared that the orchestra should support the singer as the sea does a boat, rocking but never upsetting or swamping – over and over again he employed that image.' Equally significant, bringing home yet again that in Wagner's mind the drama, always the drama, was the 'commanding form' (to borrow Suzanne Langer's expression), is the directive that when motives are repeated the manner of the repetition should depend upon the dramatic context: 'A particular remark of Wagner's I must not pass over: when the (Valhalla) motive is depicting an actual happening it should be delivered in a grand style, slowly and broadly, but when serving as a reminiscence – as for example in Sieglinde's narrative – slightly faster and with accents less pointed . . . A fine line must always be drawn between the degree of expression demanded by a present event and a recollected one.' And since drama is the 'commanding form' it must be 'a matter of principle never, except in very rare cases, to transform scenic effects into purely pictorial ones'. For 'drama is a medium through which life is conveyed in the form of life and life is in a perpetual state of flux'.

Scenic design as such only comes into its own when the action comes to a standstill (as in *Das Rheingold* after the giants have borne Freia away and the gods feel their youth slipping from them); then 'it is as much the scenic designer's function to aid the dramatist by providing a significant and gripping spectacle as it is the composer's to reveal the situation's inner meaning'. As if all this were not enough, Porges, in his introduction and as he takes us through the drama scene by scene describing the manner and the whys and wherefores of Wagner's directions, gives us more than a glimpse of what Wagner conceived to be the drama's inner meaning. What the *Ring* represents, we come to realize, is man's Laacoon-like struggle with his 'daemonic' nature, with his unfathomable, elemental passions and greeds and lusts. The supreme manifestation of this 'daemonic' nature is the betrayed Brünnhilde's demand for an avenger, 'delivered in a voice of steel: "Wer bietet mir nun das Schwert, mit dem ich die Bande zerschnitt?", which . . . drew from Wagner – as though he himself were carried away by its elemental power – the exclamation: "This is the most terrible moment!"' It is because Wagner was capable of creating a situation such as this and then by the power of his music in the Immolation scene transcending it, that Porges' definition of Wagner's achievement in the *Ring* as 'a triumph of the spirit', in that he 'was able to master the tumultuous workings of all the sensuous and daemonic forces of life and emerge victorious from the encounter', rings true. More clearly than ever we see what so many have refused to acknowledge: that the greatness of Wagner's music is part of a still greater whole.

As Wagner well knew when he gave him that commission, Porges was a man of exceptional parts. The following entry from Riemann's *Musiklexicon* speaks for itself:

Porges, Heinrich, born 25 November 1837 in Prague, died 17 November 1900 in Munich; German writer on music, studied music and philosophy, in 1863 became co-editor with Brendel of the *Neue Zeitschrift für Musik* in Leipzig. In 1867 went to Munich as editor of the *Süddeutsche Presse*, from 1880 onwards functioned there as music critic of the *Neueste Nachrichten* and in 1886 founded the Porges Choral Society which besides works by Bach and Palestrina devoted itself especially to those of Berlioz, Liszt, Cornelius and Bruckner. He was also for some time a piano teacher at the Royal Music School . . .[2]

Porges' first contact with Wagner was in 1863, the year of his vain

2 *Riemann's Musiklexikon*, ed. Carl Dahlhaus, London 1975, p. 401.

struggle to re-establish his career with a production of *Tristan* in Vienna. It was Carl Tausig, it seems, who having given a highly successful concert with Liszt in Prague in 1861, put into Wagner's head the idea of a concert there; Liszt, Cornelius and Bülow were on intimate visiting terms with the Porges family in Prague – a Jewish family, but in this context that did not matter – one of whom, Heinrich's younger brother Fritz, a doctor, was living in Vienna.[3] Fritz enthusiastically supported the idea. He passed it on to Heinrich, an ardent adherent of the 'New Music' and man of the musical world who knew the ropes: which hall to book, from whom to raise a guarantee, where to publicize. So effective were his efforts that Wagner enjoyed the memorable experience of a concert which was not only artistically but also financially successful.[4]

In 1864 the relationship between the two developed rapidly. Porges was one of the friends who arranged the sale of Wagner's effects after he fled from his creditors in Vienna; later that year, when his fortunes were changed overnight by King Ludwig of Bavaria, Wagner invited Porges not only to come to Munich as his private secretary, but to *live* there with him: 'How important for me and how beautiful always to have your understanding, friendly companionship!'[5] But Porges preferred to devote his pen to Wagner's cause – to co-edit the Wagner-orientated *Süddeutsche Press*, write a piece on *Lohengrin*, performed in Munich in 1867, and an essay on *Tristan* (published posthumously in 1906). In 1869, when *Das Rheingold* was produced in Munich against Wagner's wishes and critics praised the performance and damned the work, Porges wrote, so Cosima told Nietzsche, 'some beautiful, profound words of great congeniality'.[6] In 1872 an article on Wagner's ceremonial performance of Beethoven's *Ninth Symphony* at the laying of the foundation-stone of the Festival Theatre gave Wagner the idea of commissioning him to record the rehearsals of the *Ring*.

---

3 Not Heinrich, as Westernhagen says (*Wagner* Vol. I, p. 296). See below, n. 4.
4 'Wagner was a damned difficult man to deal with', Fritz told Heinrich. Heinrich was nevertheless bowled over by his personality when he came to Prague. Ranking him with Liszt, his other idol (he had at one time contemplated the career of a piano virtuoso), he told his fiancée that throughout his life he intended to serve those two: 'I shall not rest until I have done all in my power to reveal to the world these wonderful men and their creations.' (See the Prague musical monthly *Deutsche Arbeit*, VIII and IX, 1909.)
5 *Richard Wagner an Freunde und Zeitgenossen*, ed. Erich Kloss, Leipzig, 1912, p. 404.
6 Cit. Westernhagen, *Wagner*, Vol. II, p. 416.

After the festival the relationship appears to have been soured for a while by an article of Porges in the *Bayreuther Blätter* in 1880 on art and religion bringing in Schelling, who was not Wagner's philosopher. But it was soured only for a while. Porges not only recorded the rehearsals of *Parsifal* but trained the chorus of Flower-maidens, earning from Wagner the nickname 'Blumenvater'. After Wagner's death Porges continued to do this. When he died in 1900 – of a heart-attack whilst conducting Liszt's *Christus* – Siegfried Wagner delivered a funeral oration, reprinted in the *Bayreuther Blätter*, which makes clear how much his support meant to Cosima: 'As he stood by my father's side, so, like a faithful Eckhart, he stood by my mother's . . . when visibility was poor and some vessels sailed blindly hither and thither, friend Porges put his trust in the compass of his convictions.'

The *Bühnenproben* was originally published in instalments in the monthly *Bayreuther Blätter* edited by Hans von Wolzogen. The section on *Das Rheingold* was brought out in three issues in 1880, that on *Die Walküre* in four issues in 1881, that on *Siegfried* in four issues in 1884, 1886, 1890 and 1893, and that on *Götterdämmerung* in a single issue in 1896. Its publication in book form was equally protracted: it was commenced by a Chemnitz firm, which printed the *Rheingold* and *Walküre* sections in 1881 and 1882, and when that firm got into difficulties it was completed by a Leipzig firm in 1896. The fact that it was in 1896 that the *Ring* was first performed again at Bayreuth has an obvious bearing on why the *Bayreuther Blätter* brought out the section on *Götterdämmerung* and why the publication of the book was completed in that year. Why a book of such obvious musicological and aesthetic importance – required reading for anyone actively concerned with a performance of the *Ring* and anyone concerned to think seriously about the work – has not been reissued and not been translated before is an interesting question. When I asked Dr Westernhagen why it had not been reissued he wrote: 'Cosima relied on her memory and Wieland had the self-confidence of a grandson.' He might have added that during the intervening years of the Nazi regime the reissue of a book by a Jew, let alone a book upon Wagner, was unthinkable, and that it is only in the latter half of this century that the shadow of Wagner's influence on Hitler has lifted from

German musical scholarship. In this country the influence of Ernest Newman is no doubt one of the reasons why the book has not been hitherto translated. For all his range and penetration Newman's attitude towards Wagner was never steady and consistent; he never fully accepted what Porges makes crystal clear, and what is nowadays becoming more and more widely acknowledged: that Wagner's music, as I said above, 'is part of a still greater whole'. Neither his *Wagner as Man and Artist* nor his *Life* makes any mention, not even a bibliographical one, of the *Bühnenproben*. It was left to Westernhagen, whose stance towards Wagner is the reverential one of Porges – the stance Newman derided – to plant the idea of its translation.

This all said, it remains to consider a simple and to my mind overriding answer to our question. One has but to put another question, namely, why nearly a hundred years after Wagner's death has the wheel come full circle, why in many quarters – heaven knows how many – is he now revered as once he was? Obviously because the function of the piano as a means of getting to know the masterpieces of opera has been replaced by hi-fi recording, making them accessible to the countless people who are neither pianists nor opera-goers. This translation therefore can be regarded as a sign of the times, a spin-off from the mid-twentieth-century technological revolution. Wagner in his black moods longed for an 'invisible theatre'. Bernard Shaw (in his preface to the 1922 edition of *The Perfect Wagnerite*) confessed that, with due respect to the scenic achievements of Bayreuth, his 'favourite way of enjoying the *Ring* was to sit at the back of a box, comfortably on two chairs, feet up and listen without looking', and went on to assert that 'a man whose imagination cannot serve him better than the most costly devices of the scene painter should not go to the theatre'. What Shaw did not foresee, still less Wagner, was a time when countless people could sit at home, feet up, hi-fi recording equipment at their elbows, translation on their laps, steeping themselves in the fusion of Wagner's music and dramatic poetry.

How inferior this solitary pleasure would be to the *real thing* though – i.e. a production of the *Ring* totally effective because totally faithful to the spirit of Wagner's intentions – this book makes clear.

# Translator's preface

In this translation I have endeavoured to reproduce the tone as well as the sense of the original, the excitement of one recording for posterity the stage rehearsals of a stupendous masterpiece under the direction of its creator. Somehow a balance had to be struck between the need to provide a readable English version and fidelity to the author's out-of-date high-flown literary style. It was not always easy. I have been greatly helped by Elaine Robson-Scott's scrupulous and stimulating revision and by my publisher's suggestions. I must also express my thanks to Duncan Chisholm for the light his researches threw upon Porges' background, his first contacts with Wagner and the circumstances of the book's publication. Finally I must acknowledge my debt to Dr Westernhagen for further information for this Preface and, above all, for the tribute to the *Bühnenproben* in his *Wagner - A Biography* which put into my head the idea of translating it.

Apart from the correction of obvious typographical errors in the original German edition, the extracts from the libretto and reduced score of the *Ring* are as given by Porges. A few additional extracts are provided by the translator.

The illustrations are reproduced by permission of the Nationalarchiv der Richard-Wagner-Stiftung/Richard-Wagner-Gedenkstätte, Bayreuth.

# Introduction

The great days of 1876, when performances of *The Ring of the Nibelung* took place that had been prepared under the direct supervision of the man who created it, belong to history; they form a milestone in the efforts of the German spirit to achieve an authentic culture bearing the stamp of truth. But when we ask ourselves what the direct consequences of this unique artistic event have been, we can point to only two: the formation of the Society of Bayreuth Patrons and the performances of the *Ring* that have been given in so many theatres. These two phenomena represent two fundamentally different attitudes to art. The Society of Bayreuth Patrons is the product of a conviction shared by an increasing number of individuals that in the public life of our time art does not occupy the position which is its due. But the majority of the so-called public are quite unaware of this: most of those who flock to our theatres are driven by the greed for sensation: mere search for pleasure, stimulating or sedative as the case may be, is the strongest motive. Such an attitude to art is indecent – there is no other word for it. Nobody can deny that this is the case nowadays, and it is for this reason that the remarkable fact of the *Ring* having been performed in so many theatres and enthusiastically received in the course of the last three years affords no grounds for optimism. All the same, we must not underrate its significance: it eloquently testifies to the fact that, for all the many signs of spiritual degradation, the feeling amongst the people for what is great and noble has not been lost: it is instantly aroused when the right voice appeals to it. A response such as this provoked by a new work of art is similar to the effect created by a natural phenomenon: the forces which come into play stem from the purely sensory sphere of perception. These are certainly fundamental to all the higher manifestations of the mind, but if elemental forces are left to themselves nothing permanent can ever be created; only when seized upon by an intellect possessing

1

the highest ideals can they become the basis of great and enduring achievements. It is the aim of the Society of Bayreuth Patrons to bring this about, namely, 'the creation of a *permanent institution* for the cultivation of a classic tradition of *performance in authentic style* of *original German musical and music-dramatic works*'. Not until this goal is achieved can we claim that the 1876 production of the *Ring* has really borne fruit. For it was not just a matter of producing a new work, but of endeavouring to present it in its proper form, so providing an example of the only true music-dramatic style, virtually unknown in our modern theatres. The erection of the Festival Theatre at Bayreuth and the performances there of the *Ring* have demonstrated that in at least a portion of the community the desire to create such an ideal drama has been active and effective. For the first time, members of the public approached art in the right spirit – they did not, like the usual audiences, passively await whatever was offered, but themselves took active steps to bring it to life. Directly representative of the community is, of course, the company of artists striving to create a work of art. Such a company can be formed only when a number of artists share the conviction that a divine creative power has found paramount expression in one single individual, and accordingly regard it as their mission to give material form to the ideal images which this genius had hitherto conceived of only as possibilities. Furthermore this individual artist, divinely inspired, should feel compelled to communicate to his colleagues and through them to the whole world what in solitude filled him with ecstasy. For his work can only be achieved if he expresses himself totally through it.

This strange process was apparent throughout the rehearsals of the first German stage festival, rehearsals which had such importance for the development of the new music-dramatic art. But before describing as faithfully as I can the course of those rehearsals I must give the reader a general idea of the remarkable nature of the personal intervention by the creator of the work. His aim was to imbue the company of artists as one organic entity with that complete freedom of expression which as a rule is exercised only by a single personality. In order to achieve this artistic freedom the performers must from the outset subordinate themselves without reservation to the creator of the work, and thereby acquire that gift of self-abandonment (*Selbstentäusserung*) which, in his penetrating essay 'On Actors and Singers',* Wagner singled out as the basis of all dramatic talent. He himself possessed an amazing gift for transformation into any conceivable shape or form – like Proteus, he could, as if by magic, assume at a stroke any role in any situation – indeed, in the rehearsals of the *Ring* he demonstrated these powers so fully that it was as though he himself were the 'total actor' (*Gesamtschauspieler*) of the entire drama. This power to influence and vitalize directly by example bears witness to Wagner's affinity with Shakespeare. What is especially important, though, is that the principles governing his style of dramatic presentation were essentially in accord with Shakespeare's. All the directions that he gave pertaining to the action – to the gestures, the positioning, the articulation of the sung words – were governed by what he himself has described as the basic principle of Shakespearean drama, namely, 'mimic-dramatic naturalness (*mimisch-dramatisch Naturlichkeit*)'. But it would be a mistake to suppose that the dramatic-musical style aimed at involved no more than this. As I have already pointed out in my study of *The Ring of the Nibelung*,† the distinctive characteristic of the work is the combination it achieves of a highly stylized art, striving for the concrete realization of an ideal, with an art rooted in fidelity to nature (*Naturwahrheit*). Though everything Wagner did at the rehearsals – every movement, every expression, every intonation – bore out this principle of fidelity to nature, one must not forget that he was simultaneously handling the whole vast music-dramatic apparatus and endeavouring to convert it into a living breathing organism. He needed such a vast apparatus because his purpose was to create realistic images within the sphere of art. Only by bringing into play all the artistic powers at our disposal is such a total effect possible: an effect at once idealistic and realistic. But this goal will only be achieved when the resources of art are so well co-ordinated that we cease to be aware of them as such and are conscious solely of the dramatic action unfolding before our eyes. There could be no question then of a coldly objective, elegant, formal art – nor on the other hand of a mere over-stimulation and stupefaction of the senses. The achieve-

---

* 'Über Schauspieler und Sänger', *Gesammelte Schriften und Dichtungen*, 2nd edn, 10 vols., Leipzig 1897 (rpt. Hildesheim 1976), Vol. IX, p. 230. (Trans.)
† *Das Bühnenfestspiel in Bayreuth*, 2nd edn, Munich, C. Mehrhoff, 1877.

ment would be a triumph of the spirit, indeed the highest triumph; that of being able to master all the tumultuous workings of the sensual and daemonic forces of life and emerge victorious from the encounter.

And indeed it has been Wagner's decisive achievement to liberate us from the witches' brew of modern opera by creating a genuinely German dramatic-musical art. The essential feature of this art – the feature we think of as the German style – is that in articulation and in characterization everything must appear authentic and natural. There must never be any suggestion of false pathos or mannerism; even the most violent outbursts of passion must possess what Schiller so aptly termed a *forceful* beauty (*energischen* Schönheit). This heroic element, this character of powerful masculinity, was present in all the many instructions Wagner gave in order to secure a correct and vital performance. To witness his style of dramatic-musical performance was to feel infused by an invigorating force. What struck one above all was the sheer strength of his vitality and, bound up with this, that wonderful capacity for flexible accurate representation (*plastisch bestimmtester Gestaltung*) which is evident in all his creations and the ruling principle of their performance, affecting equally the mimetic action, the articulation of the words, the musical expression of the emotions and the execution of the symphonic passages. Yet all the extraordinary things Wagner did at the rehearsals created the impression of having been *improvised*: it was as though everything he demanded and himself so eloquently demonstrated occurred to him in a flash with complete lucidity just at that very moment. The compulsion to communicate with the utmost clarity and definiteness took creative shape in the act of expression. Fully to understand his achievement, though, one must realize that what he was striving to convey was the essence of the nature of the world, the essence underlying external realities perceived by the senses. The characteristic which stamps the style of *The Ring of the Nibelung* is that here an undreamt-of super-reality (*Überwirklichkeit*) is given life and shape, and this characterized everything the composer did when his work was being rehearsed. Thus we can conclude these general considerations by affirming that through the performance of the *Ring* the goal was achieved of combining the realistic style of Shakespeare with the idealistic style of antique tragedy; of bringing about an organic union between a highly stylized art, striving for a direct embodiment of the ideal, with an art rooted in fidelity to nature (*Naturwahrheit*). An ideal naturalness and an ideality made wholly true to nature – this is the direction in which Wagner was endeavouring to guide his performers.

Josef Hoffmann, Vienna: designs for *Rheingold*, 1876
Above: Scene 1, At the bottom of the Rhine
Below: Scene 4, Valhalla transformation

# Das Rheingold

### Scene 1

Nowhere in the *Ring* is the demand for an ideal art rooted in fidelity to nature more pressing and yet more difficult to meet than in *Das Rheingold* – indeed its production can be regarded as a test case for a proper understanding of Richard Wagner's music-dramatic style. The main reason for apparent failure in a performance of this work is that it must be governed by a vital and wilful determination, which is, nevertheless, discreetly controlled. This is the essence of artistic style and must be operative; its absence cannot be made good by warmth of expression or outbursts of passion. An instruction given by Wagner for the performance of the main theme illustrates this difference between mere display of feeling and a truly artistic delivery:

He wanted the high notes of the horns, especially the climactic G of the widely arched melody, to be played 'very tenderly and with sustained softness', and this to apply to every subsequent repetition. The players must consciously counteract here the natural tendency to make a crescendo on a rising progression; only then will the figure have the desired quality of ideal freedom. Furthermore, sustained softness will serve to clarify the overlapping deliveries of the theme in the complicated passage for eight horns. Regarding the orchestral prelude as a whole, built on a single E flat major triad, Wagner insisted that its huge crescendo should throughout create the impression of a phenomenon of nature developing quite of its own accord – so to say, an impersonal impression. Nothing must be forced; there must be no sense of a conscious purpose imposing itself. Thus the goal will be achieved. It will be as though we were experiencing the magical effects of an ideal presence; as though, no

7

longer conscious of the music, we had become immersed in the primal feelings of all living things and were peering directly into the inner workings of natural forces.\*

Wagner had comparatively few remarks to make about the first scene. The Rhinemaidens had been so thoroughly rehearsed at the piano that they sang their roles with virtuosic ease and confidence – and how superbly the Alberich† brought out the daemonic nature of this character has often been remarked upon in the *Bayreuther Blätter*. Wagner gave especial attention to the harmonic figurations of the strings' accompaniment to Woglinde's joyous song just after the rise of the curtain. They should be as pianissimo as possible. The unexpected conversion of a powerful crescendo into a piano‡ created the effect of a transformation of the waves of water into a single human figure, 'slender and light as though created out of nothing',⊕ moving freely and gracefully before us.

I will now make some general remarks about the principal features of the performance of this opening scene. Everything combined to produce a totally unified effect. The swift, impetuous movements of the Rhinemaidens and the corresponding orchestral passages were co-ordinated with hair's-breadth precision. It also seemed to me particularly noteworthy that in the songs of the Rhinemaidens, even when the flow of lyrical feeling predominated, the sense of an ongoing dramatic dialogue was strictly maintained. Only when it is performed in this way does the closed unity of the musical structure of this scene reveal itself. Here Wagner solved the

---

\* For the creation of this absolutely magical effect it was necessary for the orchestra to be invisible. In this context I must take the opportunity to repeat my conviction that this invisibility, made possible by the amphitheatrical structure of the auditorium, is the essential precondition for an ideal performance of the *Ring*. I am speaking from experience when I say that many who when they went to the Festival were out of sympathy with Wagner's ideas were painfully disillusioned the first time they visited an ordinary theatre again; they found themselves longing for that space where the simplicity left the mind free to attune itself to the mood of devotion necessary for the reception of artistic works of deep import. Another feature of the Bayreuth theatre that deserves mention is the handling of the curtain. There it is not raised as in other theatres; instead two curtains hanging side by side are swung back. This has the advantage that the stage picture, instead of appearing bit by bit, is revealed to our astonished eyes in a single instant.

† Karl Hill. (Trans.)

‡ The device, frequently used by Beethoven, of a sudden pianissimo after a crescendo is of the utmost stylistic significance in that it can be regarded – so it seems to me – as a direct expression of that control of form over matter which Schiller held to be the supreme function of art. A particularly memorable example of the device is the blood-curdling effect of the rising and falling scales in the overture to *Don Giovanni*.

⊕ Schiller. (Trans.)

problem of how to create a continuous flow out of a succession of simple periodic forms. The magical charm, touched with irony, which makes one feel that some of these melodies have an affinity with Mozart's is spoilt if they are delivered sentimentally or with a deliberate self-conscious coquetry. The sensibilities tread a fine borderline here between semblance and truth and there must be no slipping in either direction. All the Rhinemaidens' utterances must be infused with a naive gaiety – in glaring contrast to Alberich. A successful presentation of this role is one of the most difficult tasks of music-dramatic art, the main reason for this being that only through his own creative intuition can the singer find the quality of voice that exactly reflects the ebb and flow of Alberich's emotions. In this opening scene, in which he performs the terrible deed that launches the whole drama of the *Ring*, we must become involved with Alberich, we must be made to see straight into the dark core of his inner being. This can only be done through the voice. His voice must vibrate with the fire that is consuming him, the fire which in this scene is the ruling element of his nature just as the soothing water is that of the Rhinemaidens. I have already indicated that at the Festival it was precisely this character that was so convincingly performed; especially skilful was the psychologically truthful rendering of Alberich's mounting greed. The opening words: 'He, He! Ihr Nicker . . .' were delivered with a certain rough dryness of tone, the voice growing warmer and more impassioned as he is swept by lust compounded by hatred and fury at the climax of:

Fing' ei - ne die-se Faust!

I quote this passage because it provides such a striking example of Wagner's power to pinpoint every emotional nuance. The singer must not let his voice drop and must above all be careful not to throw away the vital second note, D; vital because this is the note* which especially characterizes the dwarf's desperate state of mind.

The passage indicating most clearly how Alberich should be characterized is his lament after Flosshilde has deceived him so humiliatingly:

* Forming the word 'eine'. (Trans.)

We - he!   ach we - he!   O Schmerz!   O Schmerz!   Die drit - te so traut,   be - trog sie mich auch!

The genuineness of the outburst could easily lead the singer to endow it with a quality of noble pathos; but here, and in every other such passage revealing the core of Alberich's mentality, the revelation should be that of an uncontrollable yet base and common greed. This is the fundamental trait of this child of the night, half animal, half sprite.

But the scene as a whole reaches its climax when the sunlight penetrates the dark water causing the Rhinegold to glow. At this point the Rhinemaidens' movements should match the smooth even motion of the violins' accompanying figure:

As the glowing gold brightens to its full splendour, the trumpet delivers the Rhinegold theme in C major, radiating a sublime Apollonian joy:

Wagner insisted that the Rhinemaidens, throughout the dithyrambic jubilant song in which their childlike pleasure is expressed with such charm, should make their graceful swaying movements in *front* of the gold. Every detail of the musical rendering expressed the spirit of the composition as a whole, a spirit (so one felt) akin to that of the supreme masterpieces of Greek sculpture. There was nothing cold about the performance and at the same time no exaggerated expressivenes that would have disturbed the pure flow of the melodic line and the harmonic structure. Even when Woglinde is delivering the solemn passage, touched with tragedy:

Nur   wer der Min - ne Macht ver - sagt

10

the individual feeling of the performer must be restrained. She is the instrument of a higher power; the vitally important melody she is singing must have the chiselled quality of a piece of sculpture. The tempo should be restrained in order to create a sense not of repose, but rather of suspended animation. Alberich has been watching with astonishment and he has been listening to the Rhinemaidens' exchanges. He is experiencing a profound change of heart. As he broods over their revelation of the gold's magic - 'Der Welt Erbe gewänn' ich zu Eigen durch dich?' - the Rhinemaidens have disappeared *behind* the gold. He has the stage to himself. Now his voice has a different tone: he is no longer in the clutches of a tormenting passion, but is taking a decision that is the product of his own personal will, the decision to commit the dreadful act of cursing love. His uncontrolled outburst ['Das Licht losch' ich euch aus, entreisse dem Riff das Gold . . .'] must therefore be delivered not only with great power but with very sharply defined rhythmic accents (rhythmic accents are to music what alliteration is to verse). This also applies to the wind chords that accompany the Rhine-maidens' cries. Apart from a slight retardation at:

which Wagner made in order to give a touch of individual signifi-cance to the passage,* a very rapid tempo must be maintained until the woodwind's expressively declaimed melody:

This mournful lament for the lost happiness of love accompanies the faint rustling of the water like a tragic epilogue.

---

* Presumably the touch of significance is called for by the stage-direction in the score that at this point Alberich's mocking laughter is heard in the background. (Trans.)

## Scene 2 (i)

The rendering of the Valhalla theme should convey a feeling of sublime calm. The tempo throughout should be a broad adagio – which does not mean that the span of the phrasing should be wide: on the contrary, accents should demarcate the two-bar sections of the longer periods. These accents, together with a proper grading of the different dynamic levels, bring out the inner dramatic development of this monumental tonal image which we must regard as the principal musical theme of the whole *Ring*. There is a particular remark of Wagner's I must not pass over: when the motive is depicting an actual event it should be delivered in a grand style, slowly and broadly, but when serving as a reminiscence – as for example in Sieglinde's narration – it should be slightly faster and with accents less pointed – at it were, in the throwaway style of an experienced actor delivering an interpolated sentence. Fricka's sudden outcry at the sight of the castle:

Wo-tan, Ge-mahl! er - wa - che!

is not, according to Wagner, a violent outburst but should be sung grandly. The same applies to her speech to Wotan rousing him from his dreams. Here it is very important to find the right tone: we must instantly be aware of Fricka's stature as consort of the ruling god. Wotan must start his greeting to Valhalla – that supreme example of the grand style in vocal composition – in a half-reclining position; at 'stark und schön steht er zur Schau' he rises, and at the concluding 'hehrer, herrlicher Bau' steps towards the castle. Then, while the orchestra is delivering the final D flat major chord, he turns back and comes downstage where Fricka receives him with her reproaches.

A general point of the utmost importance affecting the whole style of music-dramatic art must be considered here. The stage rehearsals of the *Ring* brought home the imperative need to moderate dynamic expression-marks, convert fortissimos into fortes, fortes into mezzo fortes etc., in order to ensure that the singers' words and inflections make their proper impact. We must never be allowed to forget that we are attending a dramatic performance which seeks to imitate reality; we are not listening to a purely symphonic work. From which it follows that symphonic passages during which words are being sung should never become excessively loud. This was a recurring problem during the rehearsals. Wagner declared that the orchestra should support the singer as the sea does a boat, rocking but never upsetting or swamping – he employed that image over and over again. Singers should not be tempted thereby to lapse into a weak or perhaps even casual style; on the contrary they should try all the harder to bring out the flexible melodic and thematic contours as concisely as possible, by means of clear-cut phrasing and precise metric and rhythmic accents. This style of performance is absolutely necessary since it is only thus that the combination of the different forms of speech-melody and orchestral melody can be grasped simultaneously. The passage referred to above:

is an outstandingly simple yet telling example of this new art of Wagner, this free counterpoint of voice and orchestra treated as equals. Two melodies, each in principle different from the other, cannot be taken in if the ear is being overwhelmed by sensuous sound. The aural sense functions as a bridge to the mind and laws of psychology dictate that the mind can act freely only when it is stimulated, not when it is overwhelmed, by sensuous impressions. Played in the style described above, the symphonic forms will be brought out much more clearly than they would in the kind of full-blooded style prescribed, often very appropriately, for symphonic works.

In his 'Survey of Present-day German Opera'* Wagner declared that if the *dramatic dialogue*, upon the cultivation of which he had staked his whole art, was not immediately comprehensible then his works were bound to be totally unrecognizable. This applies espe-

* 'Ein Einblick in das heutige deutsche Opernwesen', *Ges. Schr.*, Vol. IX, p. 328. (Trans.)

cially to *Das Rheingold*, the portion of the *Ring* furthest removed from old-style opera, of which the chief constituent was, as Wagner put it with characteristic trenchancy, 'monologue cast in the form of arias with a succession of soliloquies'. His dialogue makes its proper effect only when it is delivered at a tempo essentially the same as that of speech. Not that words must be thrown away without any attention to detail; on the contrary, employing the tempo of natural speech enables the singer to dwell on important words without lapsing into the intolerably mannered, drawn-out phrasing which makes the recitatives in our opera theatres such torture. In any case, in Wagner's works the pace of every syllable is determined by note-values; the performer has only to articulate the rhythmic structure accurately and the expression of the musical speech will be right. If he can also sense – absorb – the harmonic basis, he is on the way to mastering Wagner's new art of speech-melody combining clarity of diction with emotional warmth and vitality.

The dialogue between Wotan and Fricka, which we had begun to consider, is a fine example of how successfully Wagner carried out his principle of bringing fidelity to nature (*Naturwahrheit*) into opera. The scene also demonstrates how calmness and grandeur of expression are possible without any sacrifice of natural feeling. Fricka's words; 'Nur Wonne schafft dir, was mich *erschreckt?*'* should not be taken too fast and the final syllable must be accented. The passage: 'So ohne Scham verschenktet ihr Frechen Freia, mein holdes Geschwister' should be somewhat broadly delivered, not dragged, pointedly rhythmic, and the last words charged with deep feeling. Her next words, 'froh des Schächergewerb's', uttered in a tone of bitter reproach, form a striking contrast. Although her movements and gestures should be passionately animated, she should always convey an impression of dignity and resolution. After the lament of 'Was ist euch Harten doch heilig und werth' Wagner gave special instructions that the final:

Giert    ihr Män - ner nach Macht!

* Italicized words in quotations from the text are the ones Wagner wanted emphasized. I state this once and for all in order to avoid unnecessary explanation.

should have a heroic character, made still more impressive by the earnestness of her facial expression and her significantly upraised arm.

To Wotan's ironic reproach that Fricka herself had wanted the castle she replies in a tone of deep tenderness, touched with ingratiating flattery, that her sole concern was for his fidelity. The beauty of the melody here should not tempt the singer to suggest that she is deliberately flattering. Although the passage:

must be lyrically sung – the phrasing and the unusually detailed expression-marks make clear that this was Wagner's intention – the effect must be that of heartfelt *speech*. The style of delivery must be 'purely lyrical' as opposed to 'dramatically lyrical'; the latter style predominates again at the words, 'Herrschaft und Macht soll er dir mehren . . .', which must be energetically declaimed. Certain points concerning the stage action must be mentioned. When the violins deliver their lively, lightly mocking triplet figure after Wotan's ironic 'Ehr' ich die Frauen doch mehr als dich freut':

Wagner asked Fricka to turn away ashamed, and insisted that, whenever appropriate, her gestures should reinforce the meaning of the words. Thus at 'Dort schreiten rasch die Riesen heran' Fricka should point to the back of the stage: the gesture would have the effect of elucidating the powerfully rhythmic motive of the double basses and percussion:

15

Throughout the section in E minor, the core of which is the desperately agitated Freia-melody, depicting Freia's flight from the giants:

the orchestra played with a passionate warmth, at the same time scrupulously observing the composer's wealth of carefully indicated dynamic nuances. Fricka's cries for help were accompanied by eloquent gestures.

The orchestra's depiction of the arrival of the giants made a tremendous impression, its vast structure instinctively bringing to mind the Cyclopean constructions of the remote past. The expression-mark runs 'very weighty and at a restrained tempo' (*Sehr wuchtig und zurückhaltend im Zeitmass*); to keep it moving and prevent it from sounding unwieldy the theme played by the strings and the trombones and tubas must be heavily accented.

The restraining of the tempo must be perceptible on the second and third beats of the bar since it gives the brass motive time to assert itself. The passage should have the character described by Wagner in his article on the overture to *Iphigenia in Aulis*,* a character stamped by 'a motive of peremptory, commanding power'.† Despite the obvious differences, the two motives have an affinity: in both it is important that a perceptible caesura should delay the progression from G to C. At Fasolt's 'Zieh nun ein, uns zahl' den Lohn' the temptation to drag created by the accompanying triads must be resisted. Wotan's question, 'Nennt Leute den Lohn . . .' should be

* *Ges. Schr.*, Vol. V, p. 153.

† (Trans.)

'quite abrupt' (*kurz abgebrochen*) and casual; Fasolt's reply: 'Bedungen ist, was tauglich uns dünkt . . .' should be calm at first and get faster at the decisive 'vertragen ist's, wir tragen sie heim'. Wotan's point-blank refusal to hand over Freia strikes Fasolt like a thunderbolt. To an eloquent orchestral figure (admirably described by Wolzogen in his *Was ist Styl?*)* he reels back, struggling for speech. Then, having burst out with his 'Was sagst du – ha! Sinnst du Verrath? Verrath am Vertrag?', he finds the strength to remind the god of that higher power to which he too must bow:

These bars form the climax of Wotan's and Fasolt's crucial dialogue, at the core of which is the Treaty motive, already heard so often, which must be delivered here in a significantly accented manner. The whole of Fasolt's ensuing speech of warning, addressed threateningly to Wotan, seems to be a broad unfolding of the basic idea which appears at this moment in such concentrated form. In the course of this, 'Was du bist, bist du nur durch Verträge' should start calmly, excitement contained, and not break out passionately until 'all' deinem Wissen fluch' ich', while the bars which express Fasolt's innermost character – powerful, yet deeply sensitive:

* Hans von Wolzogen. *Was ist Styl? Was will Wagner? Was soll Bayreuth?*, Leipzig 1881, p. 25. (Trans.)

– should be held back somewhat and every word clearly enunciated. At the strings' syncopated entry:

Fasolt should wince suddenly, deeply insulted by Wotan's contemptuous dismissal, 'Die liebliche Göttin . . . was taugt euch Tölpern ihr Reiz?' His cry, 'Höhnst du uns? Ha wie Unrecht!', trembling and agitated, expresses his bitter resentment.

The passage:

was particularly well realized, sung and played as it was according to Wagner's direction, 'broadly expounded', which gave it an almost pictorial quality. Touched as we had been there by the breath of idealism the contrast with the giant's subsequent, heavily accented 'Wir Plumpen plagen uns . . .' was doubly effective. His penultimate lines, 'Ein Weib zu gewinnen, das wonnig and mild bei uns Armen wohne', should be sung very expressively, his voice and the orchestra fading out gently in the last two bars:

We now learn from Fafner the signifance Freia has for the life of the gods since she alone knows how to tend the golden apples. It is very important that the relevant D major theme should not be dragged:

Even so, the theme's concise rhythmic structure must have a certain smoothness of delivery so that the passage as a whole makes a mysterious veiled effect. Fafner's sudden brutal 'ihrer Mitte drum sei sie entführt!' dramatically heightens the tension. There is an undercurrent of fear now in the calmness that Wotan has maintained, a calmness which forms a striking contrast to the urgent demands of the giants, one of whom, Fafner, tries, without hesitating, to grab hold of Freia. As she cries for help, the string accompaniment:

should have a powerful accelerando; but this must not have the effect of hurrying the radiant Froh motive:

which conveys the exuberance of the young god protectively clasping Freia in his arms. The performance of all this created an atmosphere of great excitement. One fine point I must not pass over: when Donner threatens to strike down the giants he must keep his hammer raised high: this heightens the visual effect. The most tremendous moment of all was when Wotan with an imperious gesture stretches out his spear between the combatants, revealing his superior authority in the grandly delivered command:

The Treaty motive, striding down a scale of over two octaves, must be so delivered that the listener can grasp it as a whole. The initial 6/4 C major chord must have such force that it is still ringing in our ears when the scale lands on the dominant of A minor. Wagner wanted the tempo moderated somewhat for Wotan's solemn pronouncement:

and his concluding words to Donner:

performed more in the manner of ordinary speech.

## Scene 2 (ii)

The second part of the scene begins with the entry of Loge, for whom Wotan has long been waiting. Wagner expressly directed that he should not enter from the side of the stage but through rocks in the middle. His exchanges with Wotan should be easy, natural and unforced; above all one should be able to feel the contrast between the domineering ill-tempered god and Loge's ironic carefree gaiety. The chromatic sixths of the F sharp major theme, like greedily licking flames delighting in their power to consume and destroy:

should throughout be very pointedly yet lightly played. Wagner was particularly anxious that the tone of irony, which conceals Loge's true nature, should contain no trace of affectation or mannerism. For it is he who embodies the bad conscience of the world of the gods presented to us in all its glitter and glory. However, this moral side of his character – likewise his daemonic lust for destruction – should only break out now and then, suddenly and involuntarily, and then immediately disappear beneath the surface.

The singer should make a point of accompanying his speeches with gestures and movements suggestive of the restlessness of his nature as a fire-god. (The accompanying Valhalla music should be played in the lighter style referred to above.) Thus the concluding words of his speech describing how excellently the giants have fulfilled their side of the bargain :

kein    Stein    wankt         im Ge-stemm

should be delivered with a characteristic wave of the hand. A point to notice is that Loge should remain upstage at first and gradually move forward during the conversation with Wotan – he should do this during Wotan's speech beginning 'Arglistig weichst du mir aus'; the two should only be really near each other when Wotan is delivering – at a more urgent tempo – the words, 'Da einst die Bauer der Burg zum Dank Freia begehrten'. Froh's delivery of 'Loge heisst du, doch nenn' ich dich Lüge' should convey his intense emotional turmoil and he should step close to Wotan. As Donner, stung by Loge's contempt, is on the point of swinging his hammer, Wotan restrains him, stepping between them with a protective movement of the arm. It goes without saying that all this stage action should be exactly co-ordinated with the orchestra's descriptive passages. When Loge replies to Wotan's urgent pressure in tones of injured innocence – 'Immer ist Undank Loge's Lohn . . .' – Wagner instructed him to reinforce the words with swaying movements of his upper body. The melodic expression of Loge's ensuing speech could not be more explicit; it reaches its climax at 'in der Welten Ring nichts ist so reich, als Ersatz zu muthen dem Mann':

Wagner wanted the triplet decorating the D major arpeggio figure, based on the Freia motive, which here infiltrates the score dissolving the tension of the situation in a flood of tender feeling, to be played very lyrically, but also very calmly and evenly. Triplets he called the 'slowest musical figure' because they originated in a kind of syncopation.* In *Was ist Styl?* Wolzogen aptly described the required style and provided a number of examples (p. 35). The interchanges of the three wind groups in the B minor passage accompanying Loge's 'Viel frug ich, forschte bei allen':

must be played very smoothly without any trace of accent. It was particularly important to Wagner that the astonishment and embarrassment which Loge's announcement causes – Fricka is the first to show this in her facial expression – should be expressed by each of the gods in a characteristic fashion; by significant grouping he was thus able to create a vivid and varied picture. In particular, at the end of Loge's tale of the theft of the Rhinegold, all the gods must make involuntary movements and exchange glances as though under a spell. An equally deep impression – albeit of a very

---

* How the triplet originated in the transformation of a two-beat figure can be pictured as follows. The uneven rhythms of the syncopated: are equalized as:

different kind – must be created by the revelation that from the gold a ring could be forged that would give its owner power over the whole world. 'So mighty an object is the Nibelung's ring!' Wagner exclaimed, as though struck afresh by the importance of this moment to the whole development of the drama. When Loge adds that this ring can only be forged by one who renounces love – 'sel'ger Lieb' entsagt' – he must draw close to Wotan as the latter turns angrily away. The cellos' delivery of the lament for love (*Melodie der Liebesklage*):

must not be too loud and must bear no trace of sentimentality. Loge's vindication of Alberich:

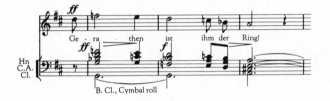

must be sung with a harshness verging on the shrill. Wagner attached great importance to the passage: it should sound like a lament for a lost paradise and yet a lament that is being mocked. He himself sang the words several times articulated in such a way as to make his meaning crystal clear; he remarked that here the daemonic element in Loge is breaking through, that in a flash he reveals his true self, then at once reverts to his former apparent good humour. Wotan's already somewhat impassioned outcry: 'Den Ring muss ich haben!' must be accompanied by an emphatic gesture. Wagner gave no prescriptions for Loge's next words;* correct delivery is guaranteed if the singer has absorbed the harmonic basis of the melody in which the finest nuances of thought and emotion are reflected. Fricka's 'Von dem Wassergezücht will ich nichts

---

* Loge's next words are 'Spottleicht, ohne Kunst, wie im Kinderspiel!' in response to Froh's interjection, 'Leicht erringt ohne Liebesfluch er sich jetzt.' (Trans.)

wissen . . .' should be addressed to Freia since it is natural that the words be addressed to a member of her own sex. As Wotan stands silently struggling with himself while the other gods eye him in suspense and Fasolt and Fafner consult aside, Wagner illuminated the meaning of the situation with the remark that now for the first time the gods realize that another power exists besides their own, namely, the power of gold. Meanwhile Loge stands somewhat apart from the others viewing the proceedings with lofty contempt.

When Fasolt and Fafner approach Wotan and Fafner announces that they would be satisfied with the gold as a substitute for Freia, the accompanying figure:

must be played with a rather pronounced ritardando and heavy emphasis. From now on the excitement of the scene mounts from moment to moment. Grouped together, the agitated gods look on helplessly as the giants seize Freia. The figure that so vividly illustrates Loge's description of the giant's progress: 'Über Stock und Stein zu Thal stapfen sie hin':

must be taken at a somewhat faster tempo, and this must be maintained at the beginning of the next section, when a pale mist fills the stage and the gods are seen to grow increasingly old and pallid. Very gradually, almost imperceptibly, the tempo should get slower, but with great care to avoid any effect of dragging. So the whole event acquires an objective, epic quality; one feels that the blood in the veins of the gods is beginning to course more slowly, that their pulses are starting to slacken; one is the anguished spectator of an inexorable process threatening the gods, casting its shadow before. The deep significance of all this was pin-pointed symbolically by Wagner's direction that Wotan must stand with his spear lowered, its tip pointing down. Only Loge is unconcerned and it is he who has the last word.

Loge's recitative-like, 'Doch ihr setztet alles auf das jüngende Obst: das wussten die Riesen wohl; auf euer Leben legten sie's an' must be sung very rapidly and freely; at 'nun sorgt wie ihr das wahrt'* he must suddenly become subdued, less impassioned, his words more moderately but at the same time more firmly and more urgently accented. Throughout the concluding 'Ohne die Apfel, alt und grau, greis und grämlich, welkend zum Spott aller Welt, erstirbt der Götter Stamm' the tempo must be strict; at his final words, 'erstirbt der Götter Stamm', accompanied by trombone chords, Loge must raise his arms, for here his utterance has a tragic dimension beyond the realm of individual feeling, here he is a prophet forecasting the fate in store for the gods. Fricka's lament addressed to Wotan has the same tragic dimension – indeed to my mind this moment was touched with the spirit of ancient Greek tragedy . . . It remains to give an example of the attention Wagner gave to apparently insignificant details. He insisted that the A flat on the second beat of the phrase:†

should not be played impassively but emphasized by a slightly lingering accentuation. How greatly this enhances the expressiveness of the beautiful phrase goes without saying.

I have already remarked on the pains Wagner took to ensure that those not actually participating in the dialogue should indicate their involvement by characteristic gestures and motions. His underlying principle was that stage action (*mimische Aktion*) should have the quality of *living sculpture*. Theoretical considerations apart, there is an important point here that cannot be passed over. The relationship between acting and sculpture should not mislead the performer into making sheer beauty of physical movement his first and foremost aim. That would be utterly self-defeating. A painting

* 'Take care to keep them!' i.e. the golden apples. The words are punctuated by a couple of forte staccato chords before Loge goes on to spell out the consequences of losing the apples. (Trans.)
† The phrase accompanies the last five words of Loge's 'Die Rheintöchter riefen dich an: so dürfen Erhörung sie hoffen?' (Trans.)

or sculpture is an object wrested from the perpetual flux of reality, thus imparting to life a semblance of stillness; it is this that enables the plastic arts beyond all others 'to make the passing moment permanent.'† Stage action has a different function: it copies reality. The essence of dramatic art is that it is a medium through which life is conveyed in the *form* of life. Since the condition of life is a state of perpetual flux it must be a matter of principle never, except in very rare cases, to transform scenic effects into purely pictorial ones. Nowadays many theatres are attempting to do this very thing and the result is a stylistic mish-mash having nothing to do with the art of drama. We are looking not for 'living pictures' – created and cultivated by elegant dilettantes, be it said in passing – but for a faithful, deeply felt *representation of life* as we experience it.

Nevertheless, in the course of a drama there are moments when scenic effects border on the pictorial – moments when after some decisive happening the action seems to be slowing down and the situation appears to be one of relative stillness. Then it is as much the scenic designer's function to aid the dramatist by providing a significant and gripping spectacle as it is the composer's to reveal the inner meaning of the situation. As Wagner cogently put it in his preface to *The Ring of the Nibelung*, the determining factor in the art of music-drama is that we are 'confronted by a scenic re-presentation in which music and poetic drama combine to form a whole in every tiny detail' . . . The scene in *Das Rheingold* we have been considering provides an example of a situation in which the criteria of plastic art exercise a direct influence on the stage picture. Because the giants have borne Freia away the gods immediately begin to lose their glowing youthful splendour. As the music expresses the feeling of mortality, so the positioning and gestures of the actors must convey their feeling of being in the grip of a magical spell threatening their lives. They group themselves around Wotan who stands brooding, eyes downcast, his spear lowered, its tip pointing downwards (as I have said). They look at him, waiting anxiously. The sense of oppression weighing upon them all is only broken when he announces his sudden decision to journey down to Nibelheim for the gold. His parting words, so full of confidence – 'Ihr andern harrt bis Abend hier: verlor'ner Jugend erjag ich erlösendes Gold!' – were deeply moving: the passage was declaimed

† Lessing. (Trans.)

with such grandeur and with such glowing warmth that now one felt the spell was lifted. The overall effect was marvellously unified, the main reason for this being the perfect co-ordination of the music and the dramatic and scenic spectacle.

## Scene 3

The powerful orchestral piece, depicting the descent from the mountain heights to gloomy, cavernous Nibelheim, was played with a tremendous weight and energy. The Valhalla theme creates an atmosphere of grandiose calm appropriate to the spirit of law and order, but now a daemonic force erupts revelling in its power to destroy the realm of freedom and love. The performance not only should but *must* be carried to the extreme of loudness for here symphonic art is sovereign since this alone has the power to represent the life-and-death struggle of supra-personal forces. From which it does not follow that it is enough to sketch the themes in broad strokes: the many and varied expression-marks, every accent, all the phrasing must be scrupulously observed, since only in this way can these conceptions, the product of a monumental art, be made to imprint upon us the features of their individual physiognomy. Wagner was particularly concerned that each entry should be made with the utmost precision and clarity. After the Loge motive rises to a gigantic power, imbued with a fury of destructive lust and yet at the same time inwardly cold, it is as though an eternal lament for the destruction of love were reaching our ears. The theme, at first delivered solemnly by the trombones, then woefully by the horns:

must grow more expressive as it makes its decrescendo. The accelerando whipping up the entry of the new motive:

was played with tremendous vigour and the motive phrased with cutting precision and taken as fast as possible. This motive (which, be it noted, plays an important part in *Die Walküre*) leads into the motive that characterizes the desire for world mastery:*

This passage, accompanied by the hammering Work motive:

forms a lengthy period, the symbolic meaning of which is fully revealed only when we look ahead to Wotan's shattering outburst in the second act of *Die Walküre* when in despair he rails against his compulsion to dominate the world:

The performance of the whole period should combine frightening power and painful agitation – as though the spirit of love in the grip of the powers of darkness were uttering a cry of anguish. The total effect of the passage I can describe only by saying that it was as though we were being plunged into a hell on earth. The scenery contributed to this: the enormous rocky ravines stretching so far into the distance that the eye could hardly follow them aroused in the spectator feelings of fear and dread completely in harmony with the atmosphere created by the music. It was as though we were facing cosmic forces of nature which mercilessly wipe out the lives of indi-

* We would call this the Rhinegold motive. In other contexts Porges refers to the revolving syncopated thirds of what we would call the Ring motive as the World Mastery motive. (Trans.)

viduals. The performance of Alberich's and Mime's dialogue was a model of correct style and vital characterization. Wagner seldom intervened and when he did it was only to whisper a word to one of the singers or indicate a tempo modification with a slight gesture. Concentrated as he was upon the matter in hand in the rehearsals he never went out of his way to display his own creative powers; what most delighted him was when a singer hit on the right way of his own accord, so that the dramatic art-work gave the impression of a self-created, living, breathing organism. In this scene what he wanted above all was a continuous tense energy; nothing must break the flow – no hesitation, no lingering – which was not motivated by the situation. In this context I must point out that this was one of the essential aspects of the expressive style for which Wagner strove in music and drama: everything arbitrary and individual, however inspired, was foreign to it. His most startling inspirations seemed as though drawn from some hidden deep layer; often it was as though a veil were removed and one had the sudden glimpse of a self-sufficient ideal world beyond the influence of any human will.

When Mime attempts to withhold the completed Tarnhelm, stammering: 'Ich Armer zagte das noch was fehlte', Wagner wanted to avoid any dragging of the tempo, and this applied to all the many passages where pauses between words provide a temptation to break the flow. He took great care over the Tarnhelm theme:

It should not be unduly drawn out; nevertheless it must have the character of a melody conceived as an adagio. In those twilit harmonies one felt the presence of a mysterious spirit-world; it was as though for a moment the eternal silence of the very basis of existence was beginning to resound of its own volition – all the more appalling therefore the fiendish and vehement energy which infuses Alberich's mockery (in a general way and in the accentuation) – the mockery of a malignant and at the same time base and common nature consumed by lust for power.

Wagner directed that the bars which, in the style of a song, introduce Mime's tale of his woes should be taken rather slowly in strict tempo:

The horn's accompanying figure should be decisively but not rigidly accented. As he tells his story, Mime must skip around gesticulating. The three figures must be carefully grouped: Loge, although his movements should be free and uninhibited, must always be in a position to play the role of mediator. When Mime's suspicions are aroused and he puts his question in a tone that characteristically reflects them:

a slightly slower tempo is called for (dictated by the melodic line and harmonic progression).

Alberich's display of daemonic energy as he reappears whipping before him the Nibelung slaves loaded with silver and gold must be even more appalling than earlier. His startled question to Mime when he sees Wotan and Loge: 'He! wer ist dort? Wer drang hier ein?' must be put with the utmost vehemence. But the climax of this unsurpassed characterization of a brutal tyrant is the moment when Alberich draws his ring from his finger, kisses it, stretches it out threateningly and then cries with a mighty voice: 'Zitt're und zage, gezähmtes Heer! Rasch gehorcht des Ringes Herrn!' After the sinister pianissimo of the bars that lead into it:

the outburst, in which the orchestra's participation resembles the Rhinemaidens' ecstatic greeting to the Rhinegold:

must be delivered with enormous weight and force, while at the same time care must be taken to observe the abrupt dynamic changes; in the last three bars the fortissimo must swell up suddenly and be sustained with ever-increasing power. It is not possible to find a more striking way of expressing the difference between Alberich's and Wotan's characters than through the latter's delivery of the speech: 'Von Nibelheim's nächt'gem Land vernahmen wir neue Mähr'. . .' The calm self-control of the ruler of the gods forms a doubly effective contrast to the savage passion of the prince of the Nibelungs. One must guard here against the temptation to drag, created by the double basses' and cellos' bare triads. The ensuing great dialogue between Loge and Alberich, in which Wotan only occasionally intervenes, is a verbal duel between enemies, each conscious of his own strength and aware of the other's purpose. The contrast between the two must be brought out in every detail of the musical declamation and stage action. Alberich's facial expression should at times reveal the threat of annihilation, welling up, as it were, from the depths of the night; Loge's features, on the other hand, should express the cheerful mockery of a superior intellect pursuing a goal within certain reach. Wagner insisted on a very rapid performance of the accompaniment – an instrumental piece conceived, both in form and content, in the style of a large-scale scherzo. But there must be no frivolous, shallow characterization and this will be prevented only if the rhythmic and metrical accents are made with the utmost precision. I should particularly like to draw attention to the passage that accompanies Loge's reply to Alberich's defiant 'Doch getrost trotz' ich euch allen': 'Hohen Muth verleiht deine Macht: grimmig gross wuchs dir die Kraft' where the rapid alternation of forte and piano must be carefully observed:

31

The precise execution of these dynamic changes, which express in a unique way the self-control Loge is exercising, ensures the audibility of the words and of the orchestral melody, the rapid flow of the music notwithstanding. Alberich must make a threateningly defiant gesture as the cellos make their swift crescendo after his 'mit gold'-ner Faust euch Göttliche fang ich mir alle!' In the succeeding bars, when the tubas accompany his 'Wie ich der Liebe abgesagt, Alles was lebt, soll ihr entsagen' with the melody of the lament for lost love, there should be no essential change of tempo. Special attention must be paid to the dramatic aspect of the passage which has the character of a free recitative:

Here, where Alberich brazenly reveals his lust, it is especially important to bring out the biting mockery of 'eure schmucken Frau'n, die mein Frei'n verschmäht' (the singer of the role did this to perfection); the words must be delivered without a trace of sentimentality – a warm glow radiates from them – but it is a glow generated in hell.

## Scene 4

After Alberich has been overpowered and bound hand and foot by Loge's cunning and Wotan's power, we leave the depths of Nibelheim. In the symphonic music of this second transformation scene the themes must be delivered with the same decisive expression and fierce vitality. The frequent changes of tempo must be scrupulously observed. In the eight-bar period:

the sudden return to a slower tempo after the 'Etwas belebter' section must convey that Wotan is calmly holding the helpless, writhing Alberich in a grip of iron. The tempo should speed up significantly – but not so that the motive loses its clarity – at the sequence of chromatic six-four figures which convey the harsh ring of Loge's triumphant laughter:

With his mocking words to Alberich, 'Hier, Vetter, sitze du fest', the fourth scene commences.

## Scene 4

We are back on the open mountain heights, still shrouded by a pale mist. Loge, in high spirits, mocks the fettered Alberich: in his terse, strikingly original phrases a unique combination of irony and humour emerges, supremely free, and the performance must convey this spirit. During the three-bar postlude:

he dances around Alberich snapping his fingers; a little later after the words, 'rasch ohne Säumen, sorg um die Lösung zunächst!', he claps his hands. Since the details of the stage action are prescribed in the score and the performers were familiar with them, Wagner had little occasion to intervene. The few remarks he did make must be exactly recorded. Before Alberich murmurs his secret command to the Nibelungs he must have prepared the movement of raising the ring to his lips in the previous bar:

Wotan must stride towards Alberich at the words, 'Ein gold'ner Ring ragt dir am Finger . . .' and take two more energetic steps when he rounds on him with the cutting 'Dein Eigen nennst du den Ring? Rasest du, schamloser Albe?' In Alberich's passionate reply, charged with impotent fury, the delivery of his venomous:

and of his ensuing 'war nur so leicht die Kunst, es zu schmieden, erlangt?' must be retarded somewhat in tempo, so that the words can be dwelt upon; thereby the daemonic power of the passage is enhanced. Wotan, unmoved, must already be beside Alberich the bar before he orders him to yield the ring: 'Her den Ring! . . .' The passage:*

---

* Accompanying Wotan's contemplation of the ring. (Trans.)

should be played very calmly and broadly, the theme rising as though with a magical strength from an initial piano to majestic grandeur. Alberich, after pronouncing his curse with terrifying power, must creep up to Wotan at 'Kein Froher soll seiner sich freu'n; keinem Glücklichen lache sein lichter Glanz!' and he must suddenly step back before delivering with fierce resolution the words, 'bis in meiner Hand den geraubten wieder ich halte!'

After Alberich's rapid disappearance, the orchestral piece, played with unremitting strength and undiminished volume until the prescribed diminuendo, overwhelmed us with its expression of the menacing evil of the situation. While the mist is beginning to clear and Wotan is lost in contemplation of the ring on his outstretched hand, Loge, with expressive gestures, moves to the background where he sees the giants approaching in the distance. At the words, 'Freia führen sie her', he comes forward again. Donner, Froh and Fricka now appear. As Fricka anxiously questions Wotan – 'Bringst du mir gute Kunde?' – she leans against him with upraised arms half embracing him. Donner and Froh remain on the hill-top and only come down after the latter's song which drifts across like a breath of spring air.

As Freia is led on by the giants Fricka rushes joyfully towards her and greets her with heartfelt warmth. Forbidding Fricka to touch Freia, Fasolt releases her himself and comes forward, leaving Freia with Fafner in the background. Fasolt's lament at having to part with Freia must be charged with emotion, especially in the last bars:

Dass mei-nem Blick die Blü - hen-de ganz sie ver - deck!

After this involuntary outburst he turns abruptly away reluctantly resigned. Freia is now drawn forward slowly by the giants; as they reach the centre of the stage the Freia melody is delivered, in this context expressive of her grief and shame:

35

The giants thrust their staves into the ground *one after the other*, each thrust coinciding exactly with the strong beat of the rhythmic motive:

The stage picture at this point is exceptionally lively and varied: in the foreground Wotan struggling to control his feelings; Loge and Froh piling up the treasure between the two staves; Fricka bewailing Freia's plight and reproaching Wotan. Soon a quarrel breaks out between Fafner, who roughly demands more and more gold, and Donner who can scarcely restrain himself. Raising his hammer he is about to attack Fafner. Wotan, thrusting his spear forward with a light movement of the hand, intervenes: 'Friede doch! Schon dünkt mich Freia verdeckt.' When Loge, having finished his work, sings 'Der Hort ging auf' he should move nearer the front of the stage. Fasolt, while he is delivering his lament: 'Freia, die Schöne, schau' ich nicht mehr . . .', at first with a resigned expression, must move down and stand to the side away from the main proceedings. Then he draws nearer to Freia and is overcome with excitement when he catches a glimpse of her eye through a chink; his voice trembles with passion as beside himself, he cries: 'Seh' ich dies wonnige Aug', von dem Weibe lass ich nicht ab!' Fafner's ruthless rejection of Loge's attempt to pacify – his heavily accented 'Mit nichten, Freund! an Wotan's Finger glänzt von Gold noch ein Ring, den gebt, die Ritze zu füllen' - must be rough and brutal. Wagner expressly asked that the forward motion of the essentially livelier tempo of Loge's words to Wotan should be strictly observed:

I quote this passage in full because it is such a striking example of how easily the emotional significance of a passage can tempt singers – and also instrumentalists – to linger; such lingering is really a form of self-indulgence, utterly unstylistic, the death of genuinely dramatic dialogue. The stage action now takes a different turn. Fasolt furiously drags Freia from behind the treasure and is about to make off with her; she calls for help; Fricka urges Wotan to surrender the ring. But Wotan, in whom the thought has taken root that it is the possession of the ring, this alone, that bestows mastery of the world, is not to be moved. 'Lasst mich in Ruh: den Reif geb' ich nicht!' he cries with seemingly inflexible resolve.

Something completely new and unheard-of now takes place. That craving for power which has seized Wotan and fascinated him with its compulsive force awakens a hidden subterranean power whose workings have hitherto been wrapped in mystery. Through a cleft in the mountain Erda emerges encircled by a magic blue light. The rendering of her warning, so deeply significant both from the point of view of the thought it contains and in the way it is voiced, was perfectly accomplished: the veiled tone-colour and absolute mastery of dramatic-musical speech accents was a complete realization of the tone-poet's intentions. At the passage, 'Wie alles war . . .', her:

must be slow and sustained; one must feel that the spirit of Erda is sinking back into itself. Her thrice-repeated 'höre!' before she prophesies the gods' downfall must be heavily accented. The last words of the passage, which seems to be closely related in mood to that of the scene of the 'Mothers' in the second part of *Faust*:

were sung in the most piercing and horrifying tones. Her parting 'sinne in Sorg' und Furcht' as she sinks down was calm, yet significantly emphatic. Wotan rushes towards the vanishing figure in great agitation. 'Soll ich sorgen und fürchten, dich muss ich fassen, alles erfahren!' should be sung in a voice trembling with emotion and with correspondingly violent gestures – this is the only time in *Das Rheingold* that Wotan completely loses that majestic self-control which he displays in all his other utterances. Fricka restrains him with her frightened 'Was willst du, Wüthender?', and Froh, after his 'Halt' ein, Wotan! Scheue die Edle, achte ihr Wort!', raises his hand in a warning gesture. Wotan stands plunged in thought, while Donner emphatically assures the giants that the gold will be theirs. Freia, awaiting the decision in terrified suspense, makes her anguished appeal. The tension of the situation is at its highest. The dark, heavy tubas deliver the Erda motive:

Wotan suddenly pulls himself together and reaches a decision:

So doing he takes a firm step and raises his spear high. As he raises his voice and calls to Freia, 'Zu mir Freia! Du bist befreit . . .', he strides majestically across the stage and throws the ring on the pile of treasure. It is hardly necessary to say how fine the performance was, how charged with dramatic vitality, how carefully interlocked each link in the chain of events. With every single performer making his or her individual contribution we followed the action with breathless attention. One small point which had a symbolic importance later must not be passed over: Wagner instructed Fafner, while he was gathering up the treasure, to leave behind a worthless-looking, worn-out old sword. During the violent quarrel between the giants over the division of the booty, Loge should move to the middle of the stage rubbing his hands with secret satisfaction as he gives his advice to Fasolt: 'Den Hort lass ihm, halte nur auf den Ring'. The giants must have moved during this to the left of the stage (to the right from the point of view of the audience). After the fearful murder of his brother, Fafner must

38

bend over the corpse as he delivers his contemptuous 'Nun blinzle nach Freia's Blick!' Throughout the Curse theme, intoned while the gods stand silent and awe-stricken, the pecussion especially must build up their crescendo to a huge fortissimo. In Loge's speech combining gentle flattery with cutting irony – 'Was gleicht, Wotan, wohl deinem Glücke? . . .' – care must be taken not to drag the tempo. How anxious the composer was to avoid any effect of false sentimentality is indicated by the syncopation in the penultimate bar of the cadence:

How feeble the passage would be if the D sharp had been on the third beat as in a Lied. Donner now follows Fafner as he moves offstage and climbs the rock. When the rainbow bridge to Valhalla becomes visible after Donner's thunderstorm, and the G flat melody is being played, the stance and gestures of the gods must convey how spellbound they are by the spectacle of the castle glistening in the evening sunlight. According to Wagner's special direction, the Valhalla theme, which now calmly and majestically re-enters, should be played with exceptionally full tone yet with the utmost gentleness. As the new theme is sounded, signifying a new deed to be accomplished in the future:

Wotan, seized by a great thought, picks up the sword left by Fafner and, pointing to the castle, cries, 'So grüss ich die Burg, sicher vor Bang' und Grau'n!' The lament of the Rhinemaidens from the river below was performed to perfection; Loge's ironically soothing remarks were thrown in so lightly – and above it all, building up a monumental structure, the Valhalla theme resounded, bringing to a close the prelude to the world tragedy about to unfold.

Josef Hoffmann, Vienna: designs for *Walküre*, 1876
Above: Act I, Hunding's hut
Below: Act III, Valkyrie rock

# Die Walküre

## Act I
## Scene 1

The stormy opening orchestral prelude, which seemed to unleash all the uncontrollable elements of nature, made a most profound impression. The performance had not a little to do with this – not only the extremely fast tempo, but the vitality and decisiveness of the phrasing and the faithful observation of dynamic expression marks gave a structured inner dramatic life to the surge of furious sound. From the very first moment we were gripped by suspense, we could scarcely breathe, and the shattering chords at the end built this up to a feeling of downright terror. Wagner insisted that the bass figure rising out of the depths:

should be executed with the utmost clarity, and the entries of the wind:

with the greatest rhythmic precision and percussive force. What concerned him most, though, was to secure a correct performance of the descriptive main theme:

'Play it with greater awareness!' he kept calling (later in the Ride of the Valkyries he made the same demand); and he insisted that the weight of the accents should fall on the upper notes. Thus charged with the full force of the creator's will, the spare, elementally powerful structure dominated the whirlwind of the artfully overlapping string entries. It should not go unmentioned that the staccato of the strings' figure as it dies away:

should be weighty, not pointed, and that this applies to the execution of the motive throughout the whole piece.

The accompaniment to Siegmund's entry had to be played with painfully heavy accents as though fighting a losing battle against overwhelming fatigue. This must be conveyed particularly in the ritardando of the last bars. As Sieglinde approaches Siegmund lying beside the hearth, the accompaniment:

must be played very quietly and slowly in order that the semi-quaver rests should be absolutely distinct. The tempo should liven only slightly at:

Here – and not only here but in general – one should not forget that a sudden piano after a crescendo is a procedure no less common in Wagner than it is in Beethoven. Sieglinde bends somewhat towards Siegmund at the words, 'Noch schwillt ihm der Athem', and after the simple, straightforward 'Muthig dünkt mich der Mann' she must not drag the first bar of:

sank er müd'   auch  hin.

which would give an impression of false sentimentality. To Siegmund's urgent call for a drink - 'Ein Quell! ein Quell!' - Sieglinde
must respond instantly with her 'Erquickung schaff' ich'. While she
goes out of the hut and then returns with a full drinking-horn the
tempo of the accompanying music must not be hurried too much
and in the last bars only slightly held back. Though the performance must be deeply felt, the personal subjective feeling of the
players must be scarcely noticeable. The same heartfelt simplicity
should inform the solo cello's extended melody:

of which the last bars bring a first faint presage of the magic of all-
conquering love.* More warmth should be conveyed by the rise and
fall of Siegmund's voice as he expresses his gratitude for the drink:

Sieglinde's impulse is to reply at once to Siegmund's earnest
question, 'Wer ist's, der so mir es labt?' but she restrains herself and
keeps silent. The change of feeling is perfectly conveyed by the
orchestra's crescendo on a rising phrase followed by a sudden
piano:

---

* I must draw attention to a stylistic feature especially prominent in the first two scenes: the
connection between the instrumental music and the silent stage action. Both are the
expression of emotions slumbering, as it were, in the depths of the soul and now on the
verge of becoming conscious. Passion, which does not yet govern the desires of the
protagonists, is making itself felt not in words, but involuntarily in a look or a glance.
Passages of this kind are most convincingly enacted by performers who make a habit of
singing the instrumental melody to themselves; every nuance of the intimate psychic
process will then be spontaneously reflected in their facial expression.

To give full value to the hesitant effect of the quaver rests, the tempo should be taken very slowly; it should be as though Sieglinde were suddenly suppressing the desire to unburden herself of an oppressive secret sorrow. The pause after the words, 'diess Haus und diess Weib sind Hunding's Eigen':

should be a rather long one since here a dramatic as well as a musical effect is intended. She hurries anxiously towards Siegmund at the words, 'die Wunden weise mir schnell!' The performance of the heartfelt, yet enchantingly graceful, instrumental piece in A major had a light, floating quality; what is being expressed here is an unself-conscious depth of feeling – indeed what stamps the musical style of *Die Walküre* is its power to convey sentimental emotions, in the deepest sense of the term, in a completely naive manner. That this should be the fundamental stylistic feature of its performance goes without saying. Wagner took great trouble over that important moment, the turning-point of the first scene, when Siegmund, after deep inner conflict, is on the point of departure and Sieglinde tries to stop him. She should be standing by the table near the tree when he strides to the door. Her cry, wrung from her by the compulsion of her secret sorrow:

must at first be desperately urgent, Wagner insisted, with the full power of the voice behind it. This does not apply to the concluding 'wo Unheil im Hause wohnt', which should be sung broadly, the initial violence giving way to an anguished vibrato. Shocked by her confession, Sieglinde supports herself with her hand on the table behind, never taking her eyes off Siegmund; then having delivered that outcry, she shrinks and turns away. The orchestral piece in D major, after Siegmund's decision to await Hunding, must be played slowly and steadily and, though tenderly expressive, with a somewhat pronounced rhythm. Care must be taken to bring out the contrast between the combined motives: between the calm deter-mination of:

and the suppressed longing of:

## Scene 2

When the Hunding motive is delivered a second time, a knocking on the door is heard. The stringendo of the passage:

must begin quietly. The tubas' delivery of the full Hunding theme must be very deliberate and decisive (as the score prescribes), its rhythmic pauses and accents executed with the utmost precision, and the players must resist the temptation to drag which is inherent in the nature of their instruments. Hunding's harshly voiced question:

Du·lab - test ihn?

should not be drawn out but put quickly; Sieglinde's reply on the other hand should be calm and unperturbed. Hunding's 'Wie gleicht er dem Weibe! Der gleissende Wurm glänzt auch ihm aus dem Auge' should not be sung with too many detailed accents. Leaning against the table, Hunding is in a position to take in both Siegmund and Sieglinde, as she moves to the cupboard at his command, in a single glance. His next words, 'Weit her traun!

kamst du des Weg's . . .' should be more in the style of recitative than song. In the last bar of Siegmund's reply, 'Durch Wald und Wiese . . .':

Kun - de ge - wänn' ich dess gern.

the second crotchet should be boldly stressed: after the previous hurried hunted outpouring, his expression should suddenly become firm. In Hunding's speech: 'Trägst du Sorge, mir zu vertrau'n, der Frau hier gieb doch Kunde', the concluding words, 'sieh', wie gierig sie dich frägt' must be violent and ill-humoured. Siegmund's anguished vibrato in the passage:

Doch weh - walt muss ich mich nen - nen.

was very moving. As he commences his account of the blows of fate he has suffered his manner must be defiant and determined. In the words:

zum Stumpf der Ei - che blü-hen-der Stamm;

a plaintive tone must be discernible, which rises to a cry of grief at the moving:

er - schla - gen der Mut - ter mu - thi-ger Leib,

The words:

leer lag das vor mir, den Va - ter fand ich nicht.

should cast a shadow and they should be delivered at a slower tempo. Hunding's manner must be grim and his expression stern as he says: 'Die so leidig Loos dir beschied, nicht liebte dich die Norn . . .', and there should be a touch of contempt in Sieglinde's retort, Feige nur fürchten den, der waffenlos einsam fährt!' In the characteristically pictorial accompaniment of the passage, 'Mit wilder Thränen Fluth betroff sie weinend die Wal':

care must be taken to avoid any hurrying of tempo and to bring out the feeling of painful lament. Siegmund's narration, deeply subjective though it is, should have an epic character. He should rise to his feet during the delivery of the motive:

and after his words to Sieglinde, 'Nun weisst du, fragende Frau, warum ich Friedmund nicht heisse!' stride to the hearth. During the postlude to the Wälsungen theme:

Sieglinde, deeply moved, rises from her seat, looks at Siegmund with compassion, and then during the rests of the penultimate bar sits down again. Hunding has also risen while delivering the speech, 'Ich weiss ein wildes Geschlect . . .' This is restrained at first, but anger breaks through as he continues. During each short pause he takes a slow step towards Siegmund; then at the motive:

he strides up to him. The details of the ensuing pantomime and of its psychic motivation are indicated so exactly in the score that here only a few supplementary remarks are called for. Sieglinde should put her hand to her forehead as she stands undecided during the expressive melody:

Having been lost in thought for some time, she appears to be making up her mind in the last two bars of the second half of the Wälsungen theme:

At the passage:

Hunding turns round and throws a searching glance at Sieglinde. The impression made by the interchanges between the three is unique. The silence they maintain creates an atmosphere of suspense and fear, tinged with tragedy. Our tension is relieved only by the quietly sounded Sword motive conveying a promise, a ray of hope.

## Scene 3

Siegmund is now alone. At first he is sunk in a state of deep brooding, utterly absorbed, making not the slightest movement. His first speech: 'Ein Schwert verhiess mir der Vater . . .' must have the character of objective rigidity and hardness; when he begins to think of Sieglinde his expression gradually softens and then becomes a glowing utterance of anguished passion at the passage:

48

Zu der mich nun Sehnsucht zieht, die mit süs - sem Zau - ber mich sehrt,

The desperate outburst:

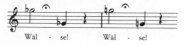

Wäl - se! Wäl - se!

should be sung on his knees, the tempo quickening slightly at the words, 'bricht mir hervor aus der Brust, was wüthend das Herz noch hegt?' In Sieglinde's narration there should be no dragging of the Valhalla theme:

and throughout the whole deeply touching passage:

mir al - lein weck - te das Au - ge süss seh - nen-den Harm,

Thrä - nen und Trost zu - gleich.

no ritardando, so that the expression for all its fervour should preserve the quality of naivety. The passage, 'Nun wusst' ich, wer der war, der mich gramvolle gegrüsst' must be emphatic, and the next words, 'Ich weiss auch, wem allein im Stamm das Schwert [er] bestimmt', increasingly firm and passionate. The transition to the following section, marked 'very lively', must be prepared by a gradual quickening of its initial bars. The performance of this whole section must express a smouldering and passionate yearning. A slight rallentando should be made in the second bar of:

käm' er aus Frem - den zur ärm - sten Frau:

since without one the expressive phrase would sound vapid and pointless. The singers must take care to avoid lapsing into sugary sentimentality in the *Winterstürme* melody which has become so famous as a 'love song': a remark of Wagner's, that the effect should be not of a concert piece but of an episode which delays rather than breaks the flow of the drama, provides the best clue to a correct performance. The melancholy yet graceful recurring violin figure which follows Sieglinde's 'Fremdes nur sah ich von je':

should be lightly floating with no suggestion of heaviness. Wagner had nothing particular to add to the directions in the score regarding the performance of the continuous outpouring of melody at this point. The singers cannot fail if they give rein to their natural feelings and are capable of voicing the emotion of heartfelt rapture. At the passage, psychologically so strange:

Sieglinde appears to have been smitten by a sudden fear preventing her from divulging a secret on the tip of her tongue; the words she then speaks should be delivered with the utmost simplicity. At his joyous response, 'Nicht heisse mich so, seit du mich liebst, nun walt' ich der hehrsten Wonne!', Siegmund must rise to his feet. Her question, delivered again in tones of deepest sorrow, 'Und Friedmund darfst du froh dich nicht nennen?', should be put calmly without any accents. The agitated violin figure:

at Sieglinde's passionate outburst, 'War Wälse dein Vater, und bist du ein Wälsung', must have a cutting edge and throughout the whole passage the tempo should not be too hurried. There should be a slight ritardando in the two bars before the grandiose entry of the Sword motive in C major as Siegmund pulls the sword out of the tree. At the close of the act the elemental power of passion together with a tremendous heroic energy carried all before them like a whirlwind.

## Act II
## Prelude and Scene 1

The trumpets' entry launching the prelude of the second act must be delivered boldly:

and all the subsequent deliveries of the motive must have the same thrusting power. Indeed, this symphonic piece must throughout be heavily accented and yet have a free, lyrical swing if we are to be drawn into the tumult of feeling to sense the fearlessness and anguished ecstasy that storm through the ill-fated lovers in their headlong flight. From the transition to C minor and onwards:

Wagner insisted that the metrical accents, i.e. those at the beginning of each bar, should have their full weight and furthermore that there should be a slight holding back of the tempo in view of the exacting heaviness of the passage and that this be maintained until the entry of the Valkyries' theme in C major:

This theme demands the same forceful, rhythmic precision which was called for in the prelude to the first act. In the final bars of the prelude:

the initial notes of the dactyllic motive had to be sharply accented. Wotan and Brünnhilde's brief dialogue should be brisk and rapid – Wotan's speeches weighty and powerful, Brünnhilde's overflowing with youthful enthusiasm. During the latter's description of Fricka's approach: 'Hei! wie die gold'ne Geissel sie schwingt! Die armen Thiere ächzen vor Angst, wild rasseln die Räder, zornig fährt sie zum Zank', the vivid orchestral accompaniment should be toned down. Wotan's 'Was Fricka kümmert, künde sie frei' should be 'spoken graciously, like a king', Wagner directed. Throughout the gripping dialogue he frequently reminded the singers to guard against the temptation to slow down in emotional passages. Fricka's speech, 'Wie thörig und taub du dich stellst, als wüsstest fürwahr du nicht, dass um der Ehe heiligen Eid, den hart verletzten, ich klage' must be harsh and at the end she must step back a little and raise her left hand in emphasis. She should not gesticulate at the beginning of the speech, 'Achtest du rühmlich der Ehe Bruch, so prahle nun weiter und preis' es heilig, dass Blutschande entblüht dem Bunde des Zwillingspaars!', but only when she reveals her growing agitation at 'Mir schaudert das Herz, es schwindelt mein Hirn: bräutlich umfing die Schwester den Bruder!' As she puts her question in tones of noble indignation:

Fricka's movements become freer and she should lean back with arms outstretched. She holds this imposing stance for some time. At 'So ist es denn aus mit den ewigen Göttern, seit du die wilden Wälsungen zeugtest?' she strides towards Wotan; her voice is hard and violent at 'Heraus sagt' ich's, traf ich den Sinn?', and at the final words of her accusation, 'dass nach Lust und Laune nur walte diess frevelnde Zwillingspaar, deiner Untreue zuchtlose Frucht' she turns away with a shudder. Throughout the impassioned lament of the ensuing G sharp minor arioso the accompaniment must be carefully subordinated – especially in the richly scored B major passage at 'wie des Wechsels Lust du gewännest . . .' With the words 'und Brünnhilde selbst, deines Wunsches Braut, in Gehorsam der Herrin du gabst', Fricka is again directly addressing Wotan, and during the orchestral postlude:

after the climax of her speech, which starts as a lament and ends as a denunciation, she steps backwards in her fury. Her whole bearing has now become imperious; her words, 'So führ' es nun aus, fülle das Maass, die Betrog'ne lass' auch zertreten', cut like a knife. She stands listening severely to Wotan's calmly delivered reply, in which the bars:

should be significantly stressed and slightly retarded. Fricka should put her hand to her forehead as she replies: 'Mit tiefem Sinne willst du mich täuschen'. At no point must she hurry, however decisive her tone of voice; Wagner was especially anxious that full value be given to the semiquavers in the passage:

53

In the sentence, 'doch diesen Wälsung *gewinnst* du dir nicht' the word 'gewinnst' must be strongly accented. Likewise the words 'Schütz', and 'Schwert' in the following example:

Wotan recoils shocked. Nearly everything depends at this point on the performer's ability to convey Wotan's feelings as he struggles vainly against Fricka's ever more insistent demands. The orchestral melody that accompanies her speech:

is the musical counterpart of his 'nagende Herzensnoth'* (gnawing grief). Fricka steps close to Wotan at the words, 'für ihn stiesst du das Schwert in den Stamm'; after the passage, 'Mit Unfreien streitet kein Edler!', she distances herself again and in the ensuing 'den Frevler *straft* nur der Freie' waves her hand imperiously (the wave coinciding with the sharply accented '*straft*'). Her demand, 'Lass' von dem Wälsung!' must be pronounced in the same manner with an almost frightening intensity, and Wotan should deliver his 'Er geh' seines Weg's' in a quavering, strangely muffled voice. In the passage:

the final note (D flat) must be cut short. Fricka at this point is once again close to Wotan. She must emphasize the first word of each of the two commanding phrases:

* Cf. Brünnhilde's 'Was nagt dir das Herz?' at the beginning of the next scene. (Trans.)

with biting accents. The tempo of her noble, deeply felt melody:

Dei - ner ew' - gen Gat - tin hei - lig-ste Eh - re

must be moderated so that each quaver of the accompaniment of triplet quavers can be separately heard. According to Wagner's directions, the word:

hei - lig - ste

should be sung with particular warmth and elevated expression, and Wotan's voice as he delivers his furious 'Nimm den Eid!' should sound broken.

## Scene 2

Brünnhilde, troubled and anxious, must draw close to Wotan as she utters the words, 'So sah ich dich nie: was nagt dir das Herz?' A truly frightening effect was made by Wotan's shattering outburst in which he expresses the pathos and anguish of his vain struggle against the moral power to which even the gods are subject. Here the most violent accentuation is called for; above all, the orchestral motive rising to a swift and furious crescendo:

and the alternating Curse theme should be delivered with the utmost vehemence. The tempo of Wotan's mysterious confession: 'Als junger Liebe Lust mir verblich . . .' was somewhat faster than that of the orchestra's preceding bars. The style of performance at this point was epic-dramatic: we should be made to feel the emotions of the narrator and at the same time to understand clearly the substance of his narration. Complete understanding can only be imparted by a performer who, while maintaining a mysterious, sombre tone of voice throughout, manages to *connect* the manifold characterizations demanded by each separate moment, so that our faculties of understanding are constantly being aroused and rewarded. Wagner himself has dwelt upon the peculiar difficulty of the task in his 'Survey of the Festival Performances' (in which he praised the consummate performance of the singer who played Wotan)*. The prescriptions in the score are so detailed that only a few supplementary remarks are called for. The rising scale of the cellos and double-basses at the words, 'mit ihm bezahlt' ich Walhall's Zinnen':

should be rather heavily accented, as though toiling painfully upwards. Brünnhilde, who has been lying at Wotan's feet, should rise as she begins her speech, 'Deinen Saal füllten wir weidlich . . .' and then at the words, 'Was macht dir nun Sorge, da nie wir gesäumt?' sink back to her former position. The Erda motive, mysteriously resounding like a buried memory welling up from within Wotan:

should be taken at a perceptibly slower tempo, forming a contrast with the preceding passage. At the conclusion of the bars:

the singer's voice must gradually die away to nothing, and by slightly drawing out the corresponding phrase shortly afterwards:

* 'Rückblicke auf die Bühnenfestspiele', *Ges. Schr.*, Vol. X, p. 139. Wotan was played by Franz Betz. (Trans.)

make the passage the expression of a deeply troubling thought. The Treaty motive striding through several bars must be clear-cut and unhurried:

and the bitter phrase:

delivered with emphasis and a slight holding back of tempo. The trombones' reminiscence of the Treaty motive must be heavily accentuated:

The extended bass melody of the next section:

should not be taken too fast at first and as it gradually becomes more animated the faster tempo should be well motivated and never hurried. Wotan's narration, deeply passionate yet melancholy – as it were, a lament sung by an invisible rhapsodist – is an expressive declamation and the tempo should never reach such a speed as would make it impossible for the singer to do justice to the manifold dynamic nuances indicated in the score. Brünnhilde, who has been listening to Wotan's passionate outbursts with ever-increasing sympathy, lays her hands on his knees as he cries: 'O göttliche Noth! Grässliche Schmach!' and looks fervently into his eyes as she asks: 'Doch der Wälsung, Siegmund? Wirkt er nicht selbst?' At the sudden forte punctuating the sentence, 'zu tiefster Scham durchschaute sie mich!':

Wotan must wince. Directly after the hastily delivered 'Ihren Willen muss ich gewähren' he should rise to his feet and Brünnhilde immediately do likewise. The climax of the outburst that follows – an outburst of unrestrained power growing ever more terrible – is the cry, 'Nur Eines will ich noch – das Ende!' A long pause, conveying a mysterious dread, was made before the C minor chord that accompanies 'Das Ende!':

The pause is the after-effect of a convulsion of feeling that shakes us to the depths, but we also sense in it a mysterious grandeur, as though a vital self-realization were taking place silently within Wotan. The contrast must be brought out between the two phrases:

The first should be sung in a tone of mordant bitterness, the second with a yielding gentleness. In his article 'On the Application of Music to Drama'* Wagner shows how necessary it is to bring out the individuality of the two motives combined in the characteristic transformation:

* Über die Anwendung der Musik auf das Drama', *Ges. Schr.*, Vol. 10, p. 229.

The first two chords of the Valhalla motive, which must be delivered with massive weight, are cut across by the initial notes of the Rhinegold motive, which re-emerges as the Valhalla motive dies away. A slight ritardando makes possible a clearly structured performance of this remarkable passage. Before uttering the words, 'O sag'! künde, was soll nun dein Kind?' Brünnhilde must rush impulsively to Wotan's side. Her lyrical outpouring, 'Den du zu lieben stäts mich gelehrt', should be sung with abandon and, especially the passage, 'der in hehrer Tugend dem Herzen dir Teuer' (during which she draws still nearer to him), with glowing warmth. Completely forgetting herself in her excitement, she turns away with a gesture of defiance at the line, 'gegen ihn zwingt mich nimmer dein zwiespältig Wort!' Wotan's reaction of uncontrollable rage quells her sudden assertion of independence. She is still trembling from the shock as she ponders in astonishment: 'So sah ich Siegvater nie, erzürnt ihn sonst wohl auch ein Zank'. The orchestra's intervention:

should not be dragged, and the Valkyrie motive:

should be played very lightly as though merely hinting at itself. During the orchestral postlude, which moves us as though it were a tragic choral song, she departs slowly with faltering steps, her spirit to all appearances broken.

## Scene 3

The faster tempo of the orchestra depicting Siegmund and Sieglinde's approach should not be sudden but grow imperceptibly out of the preceding adagio. The emotions involved, the anguish and turmoil, require a performance of the melodic figures, pursuing and intertwining with each other, that combines melting tenderness with vehement passion. Wagner was particularly concerned with the stage action in this scene since the sudden changes of position, gesture and facial expression raise considerable difficulties. The looks and movements of the protagonists must convey the wildly conflicting feelings, the ecstatic bliss, the desperate fear, which the orchestral melody is voicing. When after his attempt to soothe her Sieglinde passionately flings her arms round Siegmund's neck, they are standing in the centre of the stage. She anxiously searches his eyes trying to read his mind. After the caesura:

she starts up in sudden terror. She tears herself from Siegmund and backs away, her arms upraised. Her eyes fixed on him, she cries desperately: 'Hinweg! hinweg! flieh' die Entweihte! Unheilig umfängt dich ihr Arm; entehrt, geschändet schwand dieser Leib! flieh' die Leiche, lasse sie los!' Her anguish and horror reach their climax in the next lines delivered with the greatest possible force:

Here Wagner pertinently remarked that what Sieglinde is saying is so dreadful that Siegmund, in his consternation, stands for a long time with his eyes fixed to the ground, trying to comprehend it. At the motive:

it is as though Sieglinde were stirred by a blissful memory and her whole demeanour changes; a sweet anguish evokes the words, delivered with a moving depth of feeling expressed in her looks and the inflections of her voice, 'da er sie liebend umfing, da seligste Lust sie fand . . .' But the moment of enchantment does not last. She wakes again to the reality of the situation before her with all its terrors and is flung into the depths of despair. Here Wagner demanded accents of the most unrestrained vehemence. At the close of the passage, 'Grauen und Schauder ob grässlichster Schande musste mit Schreck die Schmähliche fassen, die je dem Manne gehorcht, der ohne Minne sie hielt!', in which it seems as though Sieglinde were holding up a mirror to her true self, her expression must convey a fearful shuddering horror. The stage action must be in keeping with these passionate outbursts. At the words, 'der Würde bar . . .' Sieglinde approaches Siegmund humbly and ingratiatingly, only to recoil again in sudden terror as she cries: 'Schande bring ich dem Bruder, Schmach dem freienden Freund!' Siegmund's reassuring 'Was je Schande dir schuf, das busst nun des Frevlers Blut!' makes no impression. She appears not to listen. Distraught by an inner vision, her eyes downcast, she cries: 'Horch! die Hörner! hörst du Ruf?' in a voice terrified and muted like that of a ghost. She sees Hunding's hounds on the rampage, hears their furious howling; seeking to avoid the danger she involuntarily approaches Siegmund, who takes her in his arms. After her stammered questions, 'Wo bist du Siegmund? seh' ich dich noch?' she leans against him at the words, 'brünstig geliebter leuchtender Bruder!' For this passage and still more so the next one:

Wagner wanted an expression of the utmost passion, throbbing with joy and anguish. The singer must hold nothing back, must throw her whole soul into it. Regarding the rest of the scene there is little to add to the detailed instructions of the score. That it was all artistically realized in a most vital and gripping way goes without saying.

## Scene 4

Wagner warned against any undue lengthening of the rests between the percussion's rhythmic figure in the solemn theme that accompanies Brünnhilde's approach:

This requirement is best met by very slightly accelerating the tempo as the rhythmic tension slackens. The broad, frequently recurring melody:

just because it is so noble and so charged with deep feeling is all too liable to be dragged. The temptation to emphasize its lyrical aspect must be consciously resisted in order to preserve the dramatic character of the dialogue. Brünnhilde's softly shuddered 'Erdenluft muss sie noch atmen' must be spoken significantly and with a symbolic downward gesture of the hand. She must react with astonishment to the final words, 'zu ihnen folg' ich dir nicht', of Siegmund's resolute reply – and still more so later when he rounds off his passionate speech with the violent declaration, 'Muss ich denn fallen, nicht fahr' ich nach Walhall, Hella halte mich fest!' In confusion, she takes a step backwards; Wagner explained that for a Valkyrie it was undreamed of that a man should reject the honour of being taken as a hero to Valhalla. Brünnhilde is encountering a new strange element disturbing her peace of mind. This manifests itself at once in the expression she puts into her question, 'So wenig achtest du ewige Wonne?' The preceding orchestral passage:

must have great weight; the triplets of the first bar must storm up to the climactic E flat with the greatest possible speed and force. In the last two bars of Brünnhilde's increasingly passionate appeal:

the heightened expression calls for a slight holding back of the
tempo. When Siegmund brandishes the sword with which he
intends to kill Sieglinde she must rush up to him, swept by compassion, as she cries: 'Halt ein! Wälsung!' Her promise to protect
Siegmund must release a flood of impassioned ecstatic expression,
vocal and orchestral. But the tempo must not be pointlessly rushed;
indeed, in the somewhat calmer episode of 'Nun rüste dich
Held! . . .' the accompanying chords must be rhythmically precise
and crisp. At the bars:

the tempo must slow up slightly, and at the repeated delivery of the
Fate motive:

the stage begin to darken.


## Scene 5

The melody of the *Winterstürme* love song played after Sieglinde's
'der Traurigen kos't ein lächelnder Traum' must be as pianissimo as
possible: Wagner said that the remembrance should sound like a
voice from another world, stirring us only faintly. The characteristic themes that accompany Sieglinde's utterances during her
troubled dreams must be handled with great care: especially the
combination of motives at 'Mutter! Mutter! mir bangt der Mut . . .',

which, though piano throughout, should be phrased with a rhythmic precision enabling the ear to grasp it as an independent tonal image. In the catastrophe that now inexorably unfolds, Wagner insisted that the rapid sequence of events and corresponding themes should strictly coincide. Every thematic entry must be given its full significance, even at those moments when the sheer volume of sound has the force of a hurricane; only this will prevent the outlines of the truly gigantic tonal structure from being blurred. A combination of scenic and dramatic factors such as these produces a unique overall effect. Because of the vivid presentation and because it is the music which expresses the agony of the situation – especially at that unbearable moment when Siegmund, pierced by Hunding's sword, breathes his last – we feel released from the shattering effect of an intimate involvement with the horror of death. Only in the light of an experience such as this can we understand the profound import of Goethe's declaration that he 'could not write a tragedy since he feared it would destroy him'.

# Act III
## Scene 1

Concerning the piece that leads into this act, the so-called 'Ride of the Valkyries', the first concert performances of which in 1862 provoked such unparalleled enthusiasm, Wagner remarked at the outset that while the string and woodwind figures playing around the main rhythmic motive must of course be loud, they must nevertheless be restrained. They should not be played at full strength until the great fortissimo when the main theme appears, brilliantly highlighted, in B major. There should be an emphasis on the first F sharp of the woodwind's whirlwind figure:

and the rhythmic accent of the strings' arpeggio:

should be precisely executed. The moment the cellos introduce the motive:

these accompanying figures should play piano and only gradually increase to a forte again. It is important to observe these directions since the music's aesthetic impression is determined far more by accuracy of phrasing than by the purely sensual effect of increasing or decreasing in volume. Regarding the execution of the main theme:

Wagner directed that the dactyllic figure (especially its first note, B) should be sharply and heavily accented since the following higher note, D, stands out in any case. The curtain rises on a rocky mountain peak upon which four Valkyries are seen peering expectantly into the background. As a thick cloud looms, Gerhilde, who is positioned at the highest level holding her spear with her left hand, waves to the approaching Valkyrie and delivers her exultant 'Hoitoho!' Wagner was especially insistent that after the B major fortissimo every detail of the Valkyries' rapid exchanges should be absolutely clear – there was nothing he hated so much as blurred, indistinct words, notes or gestures. To secure this clarity the tempo must be held back for Ortlinde's words of greeting (delivered after she has come down from the peak):

Zu Ort-lin-dens Stu - te stell' dei-nen Hengst: mit mei-ner Grau-en grast gern dein Brau-ner,

and this applies to the other Valkyries' lines. For these and all other such passages Wagner gave the characteristic direction: 'Sharply accented and of moderate force!' In this scene therefore it should be the rule to deliver all passages of dialogue (in which the emphasis is on the words) weightily in a restrained tempo and return to the original faster tempo for the more violent and uncontrolled outbursts. The stage action should avoid any suggestion of routine; on the other hand freedom and spontaneity should not lead to unmotivated running hither and thither: every change of position and indeed bodily movement must be dictated by the events. One thing especially Wagner would not tolerate was that the Valkyries should huddle together in a group – he gave repeated warnings against this, spiced with sarcastic humour. Supervising everything, he staged a scene of turmoil quite unprecedented in the theatre. The secret of the total effect – one was caught up in a whirlwind of tremendous excitement and yet able to retain one's freedom of intellectual judgment – was the perfect co-ordination of spectacle, drama, orchestra and song. After their cadence:

the Valkyries rush down to the lower part of the stage. Throughout the dialogue, 'Wart ihr Kühnen zu zwei? . . .', the accompaniment:

should be rhythmically very weighty, abrupt and rather dry. The interwoven reminder of the Valhalla theme:

must not be laboured and dragged. Regarding the action, Wagner instructed the singers to 'Step boldly forward whenever you have anything to say.' After Siegrune cries: 'In brünstigen Ritt jagt Brünnhilde her', the Valkyries must rush to the background to watch and greet the newcomer. The orchestral passage in C minor:

# Act III Scene 1

depicting Brünnhilde's flight from Wotan's rage should be taken more loudly before the voices enter, but the basses' melody must be significantly accented throughout. When the Valkyries cry: 'Schwester! Schwester! was ist gescheh'n?' they must all hurry into the pine forest leaving the stage completely empty during the F sharp minor chord. From this point the tension increases from moment to moment: in fear and trembling we anticipate what is going to happen. Wagner took great pains over the way Sieglinde, staring with cold, fixed eyes, should break her silence and in deathly tones, as from the grave, utter the lines:

He warned against delivering them too slowly; the desired effect could only be achieved by sincerity of expression. He was emphatic that every word, indeed every syllable, of her next line:

should be clearly articulated, otherwise all was lost. At this point Sieglinde draws somewhat nearer to Brünnhilde. At the words: 'O deckte mich Tod, dass ich's denke!' she bows her head in grief; then she turns quickly and looks up at Brünnhilde as she continues with increasing intensity:

The desperate outburst in the last two bars must be delivered with unrestrained force. Brünnhilde's reply:

must not be hurried, despite the more dynamic tempo, and Wagner told the orchestra to subordinate and adapt its accompaniment to the spontaneous expression of the singer. Brünnhilde's next lines:

should be unhurried and rhythmically forceful. But it was to her final line:

that Wagner attached the greatest importance. He sang it himself with thrilling power, his voice ringing with a prophetic fervour which aroused in us the terror and delight then expressed by Sieglinde after her initial violent shock. He pointed out how important this moment was to the development of the action, remarking that Sieglinde is possessed by the knowledge that she is the chosen instrument of a momentous fate. When the Valkyries in chorus refuse to give their protection (and at this point those standing at the top of the rock must bend downwards slightly):

every word and sound must be enunciated with the utmost precision, especially the incisive unison of the last two bars. As Brünnhilde asks: 'Wer von euch Schwestern schweifte nach Osten?' she looks around with anxious questioning gestures. Despite the much faster tempo of her eloquently rhythmic:

the melody must not sound hurried. The first appearance of the
theme which announces the liberator, Siegfried:

must be given especial weight, though without any perceptible
slackening of tempo. Into her ecstatic outcry:

Sieglinde must put all the intensity of which she is capable, she
must release a great flood of emotion, enraptured and enrapturing.*
Here it is important to bear in mind Wagner's instruction that even
in passages of lyrical abandon the singer should not adopt the bad
old operatic habit of addressing the public but always keep the head
turned in profile. After Sieglinde has fled, Wotan's terrifying voice
is heard for the first time and the excitement reaches its highest
pitch. In an agony of suspense we await the outcome.

## Scene 2

That tremendous theme signifying death and destruction which
accompanies Wotan's entry:

---

* It is well known that this supremely lovely melody, banishing the terror of death, is
employed at the close of *Götterdämmerung* as the song of redemption that overcomes the
power of fate.

should be played with the utmost energy. Having asked in menacing tones: 'Wo ist Brünnhild', wo die Verbrecherin? Wagt ihr, Böse vor mir sie zu bergen?' he stands leaning back slightly, striking a formidable pose. All his speeches must be forceful and un-restrained. It should be noted that a slight rallentando should be made in the penultimate bars of the Valkyries' chorus of appeal, and that here the second voice, Gerhilde's, which takes the upper line, should predominate:*

During Wotan's ensuing recitative the tempo, at first slightly slower, should speed up again at the conclusion of the phrase:

For the correct delivery of the frequently recurring:

Wagner gave the characteristic instruction: 'Always furious, never histrionic!' And this indicates how Wotan's speeches should be delivered – those threatening speeches charged with an uncontrol-lable elemental power yet infused with dignity and grandeur. At the bars:

---

* I cannot resist drawing attention to the novelty of the way the Valkyries' choral parts were handled. By following the dramatic principle of allowing each individual the greatest possible freedom of expression without permitting any lapse into chaotic formlessness, justice is done, with no trace of schematic formalism, to the musical principle demanding an overall unity. The musical ensemble-effect of earlier 'opera', combining the full strength of choral sound with the individually characterized prominence of each vocal line, was usually achieved only by bringing the drama to a standstill; here the effect is achieved without interrupting the flow of the action. Perhaps a stylistic influence may be found in the gruesome songs of the Furies pursuing Orestes in the *Eumenides* of Aeschylus.

# Act III Scene 2

Dir mein Wunsch al- lein ihr schuf!

Wagner pointed out that the tempo gets slower of its own accord (due to the more intense emotional expression). For the pronouncement, 'Nicht straf' ich dich erst! deine Strafe schufst du dir selbst . . .', besides exact observation of every accent he wanted an insistent forward motion: 'perpetually enraged', as he put it on one occasion. At the commencement of the F minor section, when Brünnhilde has to fall to her knees as she cries: 'Du verstössest mich? Versteh' ich den Sinn?', the tempo should be extremely fast. In order to avoid a laboured effect the whole section should be conducted alla breve. Wagner's spontaneous comment, 'Without any pain', regarding the delivery of the Annunciation of Death melody:

nicht weis ich dir mehr Hel - den zur Wal

is highly significant. The warning to avoid any suggestion of tenderness (*Weichheit*) instantly illuminates the distinctive character of this passage, namely, that it voices two contrary states of feeling: ruthless anger – which, though controlled, is the basic feeling – coupled with a deep secret grief. At the words, 'ausgestossen aus den ewigen Stamm', Brünnhilde reels back with a gesture of despair. Wagner was careful to ensure that the Valkyries exactly follow the instructions in the score regarding their behaviour. Their concern at the fate in store for their sister must be manifested throughout by expressive gestures. As they utter their desperate cry, 'Wehe! Wehe! Schwester, ach Schwester!' they hasten down from the rock and group themselves around her as she makes her passionate appeal to Wotan. Brünnhilde turns to them as though for help while Wotan gives his harsh reply; but at his bitterly scornful 'aller Spottenden Ziel und Spiel!' they recoil terrified, and after Brünnhilde has fallen forward with a shriek draw back from her in horror. It is important that this should coincide exactly with the orchestra's eloquent:

71

After Wotan's threatening dismissal, 'hurtig jagt mir von hinnen, sonst erharrt Jammer euch hier!', they scatter and rush shrieking towards the wood. This action had to be repeated several times before it was done with the wild vehemence, matching the surge of the orchestra, that Wagner wanted. An effect of inexpressibly tragic sadness was created by the bass clarinet's melody, which so movingly conveys the mood of the moment, the anxiety, the expectancy:

Its performance requires a blending of profound emotion with, if I may so express myself, impressionable calm (*plastische Ruhe*), attainable only if the crescendo and diminuendo are made to sound absolutely spontaneous and natural. If this is done, when the melody is repeated in the major the effect is heartrending.

## Scene 3

After a long, solemn pause Brünnhilde timidly raises her head a little. The bass clarinet's phrase, which so expressively illustrates the gesture:

must be played with a slight touch of hesitation and delay. During her moving speech – so heartfelt, so naively submissive – she must gradually raise herself to a kneeling position, so that when she reaches the final bars:

zu ver - stos - sen dein trau - te - stes Kind?

she is able to lean back in a gesture appropriate to the heightened emotion of the phrase. At the words: 'als Fricka den eigenen Sinn dir entfremdet', she is standing. Wotan's question, 'Du wusstest es so, und wagtest dennoch den Schutz?' must have something of the character of a sudden outburst, without being too passionate. Regarding the consistently reiterated semiquaver figure:

Wagner directed that, its expressiveness notwithstanding, it should not be dragged; and regarding the phrase intertwined and alternating with it in a duet-like fashion:

that the sextolets should not be emphasised, but that the dotted notes should be slightly accented.* Generally speaking, the tempo should be held back rather than driven forward; this must be borne in mind particularly at Brünnhilde's words: 'Die im Kampfe Wotan den Rücken bewacht, die sah nun Das nur, was du *nicht* sah'st'. Throughout her impassioned speech describing how the depth of her sympathy with Siegmund drove her to break Wotan's command and protect him, Wotan stands unmoved, his head averted. The tone of his reply, 'So thätest du . . .', is at first stern and sombre; but when the god speaks of his own fearful mental torment his utterance is elevated to an intense expression of noble anguish. The after-effect of this tremendous moment, the fateful Curse theme:

* In the vocal score the sextolet figure is altered to make it more playable.

had to be given its due significance and yet played steadily. The chordal accompaniment of Wotan's moving passage, 'So labte süss dich selige Lust . . .' should be as pianissimo as possible and respond closely to the expression of the singer. Wagner wanted Brünnhilde's words, 'Du zeugtest ein edles Geschlecht, kein Zager kann je ihm entschlagen', half-whispered as though she were imparting an intimate secret, to be shrouded in mystery; the Wälsungen motive, sounded at that point:

must be brought out very clearly and this means that the soft muted delivery must be phrased with the utmost rhythmic incisiveness. This also applies to the voice and orchestra's somewhat louder delivery of the Siegfried theme:

during which Brünnhilde must draw nearer to Wotan. His abrupt response, 'Schweig mir vom Wälsungenstamm!' must be delivered with considerable violence. Wagner insisted that Brünnhilde's articulation of the words:

should make their meaning absolutely clear. Wotan's violent exclamation, 'Und dass ich ihm in Stücken schlug!' must be accompanied by an aggressive gesture. Brünnhilde falls to her knees in despair at Wotan's words, 'Zu viel begehrst du, zu viel der Gunst'. She wrings her hands, drags herself across the ground and embraces his knees as she implores: 'Dies Eine nur musst du erhören! . . .' For the final words of that plea:

Doch    gieb,    Grau  -   sa - mer, nicht der gräss  -   lich-sten Schmachsie preis!

Wagner demanded the most extreme intensity of expression. Brünnhilde then falls back on to a small hillock. But what Wagner took
especially great trouble over was the symphonic passage in E major
when Brünnhilde sinks on Wotan's breast and he holds her in a
long embrace. 'It must be a work of art', he declared from the
outset. The first two bars:

were very controlled and the powerful mounting crescendo created
an effect of elevated grandeur. It was essential that the percussion
should be fairly prominent. The woodwind's sequentially extended
continuation of the main motive, played with glowing warmth:

had the character of an expressive song swelling triumphantly to
the supreme fortissimo:

Highly significant is Wagner's remark apropos of the fifth bar where
the melody lands on the dominant, B: 'Here the knot of the tempo
loosens', by which he meant that at this point the metric-dynamic
tension reaches its highest pitch and that thereafter the expression
must gradually relax and grow calm. This calm should form the
ground-tone of Wotan's moving farewell: despite its moments of passionate intensity it should never quite lose its elegiac quality. Words
and music here must be on an equal footing. The deep, conceptual

significance of the god's speech must imprint itself on our minds without disturbing the flow of lyrical feeling. The bridge between the two factors is the rhythmic articulation, which at this point is sufficiently varied to make possible a combination of the most melting tenderness and an expression of heroic grandeur. The flow of the accompanying obbligato figure:

must be calm and even at the beginning, and when the melody becomes impassioned still always subordinate to the singer. The tempo must be strict at first in the passage:

The rallentando that starts in the second bar and continues to the end of the phrase must be very steady and gradual, determined by the weight of the accents. A remark of Wagner's that has an important bearing on the action must be cited: at the words, 'Denn so kehrt der Gott sich der ab, so küsst er die Gottheit von dir', one must for the first time see Wotan's spear slipping from his hand.

At the bars:

Wotan starts up suddenly and then, as the Treaty motive is sounded, strides slowly and solemnly to the middle of the stage. Regarding the magic fire music Wagner warned that the crescendo and the involuntarily quickening tempo should cease after the two-bar sequence of chromatic sixths:

and in the ensuing bars the music must regain its original poise. Particular care must be taken to give an accurate rendering of the notes of lesser time-value in the monumental delivery of the Siegfried theme:

Regarding the melodic pendant to that theme:

in which the composer solved the problem of how to express deep emotion in a style of calm sublimity, Wagner insisted that the tempo should not be hurried: the speed should be such that each semiquaver of the harps' accompanying figure:

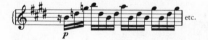

should be clearly perceptible. Due weight must be given to the Fate motive, surging up from the depths, posing its eternal question:

before the final, blissful resolution into E major.

Josef Hoffmann, Vienna: designs for *Siegfried*, 1876
Above: Act I, Mime's cave
. Below: Act III, At the foot of Brünnhilde's rock

# Siegfried

## Act I
## Scene 1

The performance of the prelude to the first scene demands the greatest care, since the peculiar character of the piece can only be made intelligible by scrupulous observation of every accent and dynamic marking. The sombre uncanny atmosphere – the very first drum roll creates a sense of standing on uncertain, shifting ground – is evoked by themes from the Nibelheim scene of *Das Rheingold*. But, whereas there those themes conveyed the force of a willpower surging from hidden depths, here they convey acutely conscious psychological processes of a very peculiar kind: the malignant dwarf, Mime, is in the grip of uncontrollable forces with which he cannot deal and so his mind is in a painful state of doubt and turmoil. Only by attending to every detail – particularly the numerous crescendos dissolving into piano – can the players bring out the dual character of this mysterious piece of tone-painting, the depiction of a being whose will is impelled by forces of irresistible power and yet confounded by weakness and irresolution.

The powerful bars, compounded out of the motives of brooding and lust and the ceaselessly hammering Work motive, which express Mime's longing for world-dominion:

form the climax of the rising progression of the previous periods. Thereafter the psychological process changes character: the mood of contemplation gives way to an agitated craving working itself into a state bordering on madness. It was precisely in passages such as these that Wagner insisted upon the utmost clarity of phrasing. Each one of the syncopated woodwind phrases:

should be clearly demarcated. Each begins piano and ends in a crescendo; thus the beginning of each phrase must be clearly differentiated from the preceding phrase. In Mime's soliloquy the temptation to drag the passage:

created by the emphasis of the words and the heavy scoring (bass tubas) should be resisted. At the moment when Mime desperately resumes his hammering:

Wagner indicated that the tempo should not be too slow, and indeed it is obvious that the tempo must be reasonably fast if the passage, consisting of two four-bar periods of trochaic rhythm ( ♩♩ ) above a descending bass line, is to be grasped as a whole. In general I should like to point out that there is no better test of a correct tempo than to enquire whether phrases and periods which belong together according to their sense are grasped by the listener as an intelligible whole.

Regarding the stage action it remains to add that when Mime recoils in terror before the bear which Siegfried drives at him he must not give the impression of having lost his self-control.

Musically and dramatically the only way to deliver Siegfried's youthfully exuberant utterances is with complete spontaneity and naturalness of expression. The performer however should guard against portraying this naturalness simply by letting himself go in a carefree, indifferent fashion. That would completely fail to solve his problem. Siegfried should not create the impression of a character drawn with the conscious intention of violating the standards of civilized society; everything he says and does – even the rather crude aspects of his genuine boyishness – must be presented as the natural expression of an essentially heroic personality who has not yet found an object in life worthy of his superabundant strength. If heroic energy is brought out as Siegfried's predominant trait – which is not to say that he lacks a corresponding depth of sensibility – then, even at moments when apparently quite ordinary events are being enacted, we shall always feel ourselves in the presence of elevated art. This is the soil from which springs that new style, in which the ideal is permeated by fidelity to nature – that new style which constitutes the originality of the Nibelung trilogy in the history of art.

The rendering of the passionately excited G minor section – beginning when Siegfried shatters the sword Mime has forged – was powerfully energetic and yet to an equal degree light and playful. This combination of such contrasting characteristics was achieved by exaggerating the accents that divide the apparently even, hammering quavers of the twelve-bar period:

into successive sections of two two-bar periods, four one-bar periods and two two-bar periods, a style of execution in any case implied by the 'molto staccato' prescribed in the score. When, at Siegfried's words, 'Schwatzt mir von Riesen . . .', a new motive introduces a fresh rhythm:

the accents, though still incisive, should be lightened. In the accompaniment to Mime's reply ['Nun tob'st du wieder wie toll . . .'], which serves as a coda to the entire section:

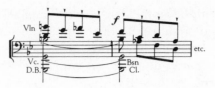

the tempo should not be retarded at first; apart from this, Wagner made the important observation that throughout the repetitions of the quaver figure* the strong beats should not be more emphasized than the weak ones. It was precisely by following this directive that the specific character of this latter part of the passage, the relaxing of the tension, was brought out. The numerous tempo changes when Mime is making his attempts to calm Siegfried down should be very carefully observed. A slower tempo should never be so slow as to convey a feeling of actual calm – this particularly applies to the rallentando throughout the fourteen bars of Mime's speech beginning 'Doch speisen magst du wohl?'. Wagner's demand – not prescribed in the score – for a rallentando in the four bars that round off the scene:

is in my opinion essential. This rallentando, which must not be exaggerated, should, furthermore, be prepared by Mime's lament of the two preceding bars, 'Das ist der Sorgen schmählichster Sold!' Siegfried springs to his feet after the increasingly fierce tirade: 'Seh' ich dir erst mit den Augen zu, zu übel erkenn' ich, was alles du thust', and, after his mockery of the dwarf's grotesque gait, violently assaults him. The lovely melody with its intimations of an ideal not yet realized:

\*  (Trans.)

should sound 'as though out of a dream', Wagner said. And when
a little later it recurs in D minor:

he wanted the mysteriously veiled choral-instrumental passage to be
played 'without any feeling, as though coming from a distance'. It is
precisely passages such as this, calling not for overwhelming expression of feeling but for conscious control, that give musicians the
opportunity to display artistic mastery. When Mime interrupts
these emanations from another world, his speeches should be in
strict tempo, without any dragging, in order to preserve the
character of dialogue. The subsequent development of the melody
in D major:

should be somewhat fuller in tone, though the basic dynamic level
should throughout be piano. The woodwind figures above the main
melody:

should be played very gently. When the bassoons enter they should
be a little louder and made more significant by slightly delayed
accentuation:

Wagner warned against the temptation to put too much feeling into
the more impassioned melody of the passage:

At Siegfried's 'Nun kam ich zum klaren Bach' the serenity and still-ness of nature was most effectively depicted in the accompaniment, thanks to the calm, even delivery (not that this precluded those dynamic shadings, occasioned by the rise and fall of the melodic line, which are the prerequisite of meaningful phrasing). In regard to the recurring G minor section, containing what must be con-sidered the principal theme of the whole scene, what has already been said applies again, except that here the dramatic action – Siegfried seizes Mime by the throat as he puts the question, 'Wer war mir Vater und Mutter?' – demands an outburst of uninhibited rage. Wagner couldn't have too much made of the two sudden molto crescendos in the quaver figure:*

'Out, you basses! (Heraus die Bässe!)', he cried, as he spurred the players on to make their accents more and more exaggerated. The accompaniment to Mime's sad tale of Sieglinde gives the wind instruments the opportunity to display their mastery of a de-clamatory-lyrical style. When those tender, anguished melodies familiar from *Die Walküre* re-enter, the fine distinction must be pre-served between the degree of expression demanded by a present event and that demanded by a recollected one. Very important, to my mind, is Wagner's direction that Siegfried must make a slightly convulsive movement at every delivery of the motive referring to Sieglinde:

'The sentimental passages only affect Siegfried' was what he actually said. The *a tempo* at Mime's 'Als zullendes Kind':

---

* Before Mime's 'O undankbares Kind!' and his 'Nicht bin ich Vater dir'. (Trans.)

should not be taken slowly and should be somewhat hurried in the last two bars when Siegfried interrupts. Careful attention must be paid to the handling of the glaring contrast between Siegfried's increasingly urgent passionate questions concerning his father and mother and Mime's petty attempts to pacify and make excuses. However, the composer's expression-marks define his intentions so exactly that the performers have only to observe them and the scene is brought to life. When Siegfried interrupts with his violent 'Still mit dem alten Staarenlied!' he jumps up. And then when he realizes what must be done with the splinters of the sword he is swept by a whirlwind of enthusiasm. The eight-bar period, launched by the jubilant Sword motive that accompanies Siegfried's exultant 'Und diese Stücken sollst du mir schmieden, dann schwing' ich mein rechtes Schwert!' must be played with fiery energy in one broad stroke. Richard Wagner himself in his unforgettable rendering of the Ninth Symphony in 1872 provided the model for the performance – the feeling of a vast sound-complex surging towards its goal – in the way he conducted the shattering trumpet fanfare of the introduction to the finale. Regarding the principal rhythmic motive:

it is self-evident that the two bars form a single unit and hence that the beginning of each unit must be accented. Furthermore at this point* the melodic accents of the accompaniment coincide exactly with those of the words, which does not always happen or need to happen. Thereafter everything should be taken more lightly with less volume; this particularly applies to the sequence based on the Sword motive:

which drew from Wagner the illuminating remark, 'It should almost have the character of a comic opera.' Siegfried's jubilant 'Aus dem Wald fort, in die Welt zieh'n: nimmer kehr' ich zurück!' demands

* At 'Eile dich, Mime! Mühe dich rasch' (Trans.)

no specific direction. Great energy and freedom of expression on the part of the singer must be combined with an accompaniment in which the beginnings of all the related sections are accurately and incisively emphasized, otherwise the contrapuntal combinations just before the end will be unintelligible. As Siegfried storms off into the forest Mime runs after him in alarm crying: 'Halte! Wohin? . . .', but, realizing he cannot stop him, he quickly turns back. The symphonic piece that accompanies Mime's soliloquy is a master-piece of psychological characterization in the way that the mood of what has just been experienced is dissolved and the transition made to the entry of the Wanderer; its performance demands a penetrating understanding of every tiny detail. Everything here is significant and important. One must feel both the confusion of Mime's mind, plagued by uncontrollable forces, and the dwarf's degraded lust for power. The gradual quickening of the tempo must have the effect of a frenetic agitation, and the motive of eternal world-tragedy, first heard from Wotan in *Die Walküre*, and now repeated three times with a broad ritardando, should be delivered with the utmost power and grandeur while Mime desperately wails: 'des Nibelungen Neid, Noth und Schweiss nietet mir Nothung nicht!'

## Scene 2

The symphonic accompaniment of the great dialogue between Mime and the Wanderer was an object of special concern. Wagner insisted that a performance of this music – solemn, yet in a con-tinuous state of flow, without tension – should combine the forward movement of an andante with the repose of an adagio. This can be done by ensuring that metric and rhythmic accents are given their due without being made sharply. This is easy enough for strings, but very difficult for trumpets, trombones and tubas. And for these a further requirement is made by the sequential progression:

They must reduce their tone somewhat at the end of each of the two-bar periods. Since the musical speech of the singers is always the dominant factor, Wagner repeatedly stressed that the basic level of tone should be piano and small crescendos reduced to a minimum. Mime, whom the appearance of the Wanderer at once throws into a state of uneasiness, draws back somewhat at the speech, 'Spürtest du klug . . .' The Wanderer, while he is saying: 'was ihm frommte, liess sich erfragen . . .', strides forward but in a manner calm and restrained. After Mime's frightened dismissal, 'Dir Weisem weis' ich den Weg', he strikes his spear on the floor to the accompaniment of a fortissimo delivery of the Treaty motive and then seats himself by the hearth. When the motive is repeated in D flat major, Mime, who was at first puzzled, is violently startled. According to Wagner's instruction the basses' sudden delivery of the Work motive a few bars later:

should be so graphic as to be positively comic. The Wanderer should, by raising his arm and stressing the words, 'der sollte die Welt ihm gewinnen', give this passage a significant emphasis. Throughout the whole scene every gesture and intonation should convey on the one hand the Wanderer's impressive calm and on the other Mime's insecurity, thinly veiled by cunning and astuteness. The delivery of the Giants' motive, though piano throughout, must be weighty (the correct manner of its performance has already been discussed in the chapter on *Das Rheingold*). In the subsequent bars:

the tempo should be somewhat faster; the main tempo – not too slow – is restored by the Fafner motive:

Of the bars that accompany Mime while he is cogitating:

Wagner declared that they couldn't be taken too mysteriously. Mime, as he humorously put it, is so pleased with his quasi-antiquarian philological knowledge that he delightedly rubs his hands. The cellos must emphasize the upper note of their scale of descending octaves, which leads to the entry of the Valhalla theme:

in order to bring out its lyrical character. As he so often did, Wagner warned against dragging the Valhalla theme – here the case in point was the tendency to drag the four bars marked 'poco crescendo' followed by a sudden piano.* The staccato semiquavers of the figure:

must have tremendous thrust and precision; the double basses especially should guard against converting dotted notes into triplets:

Even when a level volume is prescribed for the tubas' and trumpets' repeated chords:

* At 'Licht–Alberich, Wotan, waltet der Schaar'. (Trans.)

their tone should still be somewhat inflected. At 'ewig gehorchen sie alle des Speeres starkem Herrn', the Wanderer rises from his seat and the tempo of the accompanying eight-bar period:

quickens slightly. The chords here, though weighty, must be lighter than those in the preceding bars. Mime must visibly quail at Wotan's threat to demand his head as forfeit. The Wälsungen theme, sounded here so mysteriously:

though its accents should have a heavy troubled quality, must not be taken too slowly. In all reminiscent passages of this kind it is the symbolic significance that matters and this can only be conveyed if the performance is not overburdened with the expression of immediate events, but imparts the quality of remembered ones welling up within the mind. The bars:

must be perceptibly drawn out by the singer and orchestra. When the Wälsungen theme is repeated at Mime's 'Die Wälsungen sind das Wunschgeschlecht . . .', it should be somewhat faster, essentially preserving the more animated tempo of the preceding bars. At 'Siegfried zeugten sie selbst', Mime raises his finger significantly; the bars immediately afterwards:

must be played with an accelerando. Mime is beside himself with joy at having dealt so successfully with the Wanderer's questions. Regarding the extensive, pithy scherzo:

Wagner expressly warned against too feverish a tempo. Every item in the succession of periods must be individually characterized – albeit without any hint of mannerism, or witticism. Wagner repeated the warning not to hurry at the modulation to D minor when the Wanderer bursts out laughing. In his ensuing 'Der Witzigste bist du unter den Weisen', the forte of each entry of the theme.

should be instantly converted into a piano. The brilliantly heroic Sword motive, which follows the Wanderer's 'Nur wer das Fürchten nie gelernt':

should not be hurried but delivered with a full consciousness of its symbolic significance. At the bars:

Mime starts to tremble. The tempo here is rather more animated, but on no account to be taken fast.

## Scene 3

Great care must be taken over the accompaniment to Mime's soliloquy, which opens this scene. Here the composer is expressing something which music has never before expressed so specifically:

an overwhelming dread of daylight. Mime is frightened by the mysterious, incessant rustling in the sunlit depths of the forest. Above all it is important that this music, based on Loge's motives, should not be taken too fast; the characteristic profile of the motives should not be obscured in the colour and glitter of the orchestration. Very important in my view is Wagner's direction that the crescendo after Mime's 'was säuselt und summ't, und saus't nun gar?' should be sustained as long as possible. The various articulations of the bass tuba's melody (the Fafner motive):

should be played lyrically – the half-gruesome, half-comic effect the composer was aiming at depends on this.

For the subsequent dialogue between Siegfried and Mime, Wagner gave no special direction supplementing those stated so exactly in the score. The orchestral setting often calls for a delicate and poetic treatment but with no excessively subjective emotion – I have in mind the lyrical passages for the cellos, horns and oboes.* From the moment when Siegfried takes the decision to re-forge the broken splinters of the sword himself the performance must be in the grand style. Therefore Wagner repeatedly insisted that the execution of this music, expressing the upsurge of a powerful life force, must not be hurried. What he had in mind was the extensively developed figure:

and the twice-interpolated Work motive:

After the forte at:

---

* Their deliveries of the Sleep motive after Mime's 'Fühltest du das noch nicht, das Fürchten blieb dir noch fremd.' (Trans.)

there should be an immediate reversion to piano as Mime acknowledges: 'Mit dem Schwerte gelingt's, das lern' ich wohl'. Siegfried's songs that now follow, in which simple Lied-forms are charged with an intensity so powerful that individual expression is raised to the level of the universal, must be delivered broadly and boldly. Therefore Wagner did not dwell on details: the overwhelming influence of his actual presence, of his wishes expressed in his looks and gestures, secured the desired effect, an effect that could be summed up by saying its predominant feature must be a massive strength. To bring out this quality it is not enough to produce sounds of exceptional loudness. What is absolutely essential is that the motion of the music should be curbed and this restraint should be applied, often scarcely consciously, to every detail of each figure. The so-called Forging Song in D minor exemplifies this. The accompanying figure:

must be heavily accented and there must be a perceptible holding back in the basses' counterpointing sequence:

There may also be a slight reduction of tempo in the bars:

though this will only be effective if the singer's expression has the appropriate weight. It goes without saying that the subsequent orchestral figure:

92

and the woodwind's broken arpeggios:

must be both brilliant and effortless. The trumpets' imitation of the vocal line:

requires particularly emphatic accents, though the 'piano' must be carefully observed. The triumphant entry of the Sword motive:

at the words, 'Bald schwing' ich dich als mein Schwert' must be significantly faster. Wagner did not want the semiquaver triplet at 'Starr wird er und steif':

taken too slowly despite the marking 'measured, almost slow'; it should retain something of its dashing fanfare character. The richly rhythmic figure:

should be played very lightly, stressing the scherzo-like quality of the third bar. The fullest possible weight and power must be concentrated in the performance of the Forging Song from the first moment it appears. Right from the opening orchestral bars:

far from any loss of tone, there must be a steady increase in intensity. The main tempo must be strictly observed for Mime's aside, 'Er schafft sich ein scharfes Schwert', with its accompanying motive:

At the entry of the Work motive before Mime's 'Den der Bruder schuf, den schimmernden Reif':

Wagner warned against exaggerating the faster tempo. The climactic outburst of heroic joy at the close of the act is composed in such a way that to bring it off the players have only to let themselves be borne along by the stream of jubilant sound.

## Act II
### Scene 1

'Sluggish and dragged': so runs the expression-mark to the prelude of this act which creates such an uncanny impression; this effect can only be achieved if the second and third beats of the Giants' motive:

are somewhat retarded and the fundamental tempo steadily adhered to in the intervening bars. It is also very important to follow Wagner's demand for a lyrical rendering of the contrabass tubas' Fafner melody.* The syncopation of Alberich's World Mastery motive [see. p. 30], appearing here like the emanation of a troubled dream, must be incisive and prominent. When the theme which we know as that of Alberich's curse in *Das Rheingold* is twice repeated sequentially:

the urgent impassioned character of the passage demands a correspondingly faster tempo; this makes all the more effective the prescribed slower tempo for the Giants' motive that follows (at this point the percussion should take note of the direction in the score not to hurry). Immediately before Alberich's words, 'Banger Tag, bebst du schon auf?', a flash of light is seen through the thick foliage of the forest. The melody and rhythm of the next section, familiar to us from *Die Walküre*, must be firmly accented throughout. The trombones' delivery of the Curse motive must be significantly emphasized, but the tone must be restrained; the horns, when they deliver the motive, must introduce a slight crescendo:

Alberich must appear to be governed by an uncontrollable fury which is nevertheless contained and manifests itself only in fitful violent outbursts: thus Wagner did not want his apparently calmer passages, for example the speech, 'Doch wo du schwach bist, blieb mir auch nicht verborgen', taken more slowly. The Wanderer's spiritual superiority, touched with humour, forms a striking contrast. The sequence built out of the Treaty motive:

95

should have a taut, propulsive ('straff vordringendem') tempo: Wagner exhorted the players to 'keep it moving!' Alberich proclaims his fearful 'Der Welt walte dann ich!' with the utmost violence and during the theme, played with a vigorous crescendo:

he makes a gesture of triumphant defiance which he holds for a moment.

The Wanderer takes a slow step forward before making his reply, 'Deinen Sinn kenn' ich wohl . . .', accompanied by a movement of the hand calmly waving him aside. Wagner did not have anything special to say about the Wanderer's utterances. It is clear that they convey a calm dignity blended with a superior, at times rather mocking, irony. In this last respect, the passage, 'Ich lass' dir die Stätte, stelle dich fest' is particularly revealing: the words here must be spoken so lightly - thrown off, as it were - that the listener is hardly aware of them as music. The powerful piece (combining the Wanderer's theme with the accompanying figure of the Ride of the Valkyries) that depicts the Wanderer's stormy departure:

should be played in a strict tempo which, even during the melody from *Die Walküre*:

must not be relaxed, so that we have the feeling that Wotan's memory of Brünnhilde is a purely inner psychic event (*ein rein innerlicher Seelenvorgang*). After Alberich's taunting 'Doch lacht ihr zu, ihr leichtsinniges, lustgieriges Göttergelichter!', the twice-repeated Curse theme is delivered by the trombones, then by the tubas: the tubas should play it with a very slight rallentando, louder but with a more conscious emphasis, so that in the diminuendo it retains its significance. This ensures that the fortissimo appearance of the theme at Alberich's parting words, 'So lang das Gold am Lichte glänzt, hält ein Wissender Wacht', has its proper symbolic effect.

## Scene 2

The Forging Song motives that accompany Siegfried and Mime's entry should be rhythmically precise but less energetically accented. The psychologically subtle transformation of the Sleep motive from *Die Walküre* into an expression of intoxicating rapture should be played with feeling, but not exaggerated. The tempo should be held back slightly for the shuddering tremolando:

which accompanies Mime's words, 'Glaube, Liebster, lernst du heut' und hier das Fürchten nicht'. At the conclusion of Siegfried's speech, begun in calmly decisive tones, 'Nothung stoss ich ihm erst in die Nieren, wenn er dich selbst mit hinweg gesoffen', the tempo should be somewhat more animated, but the expression should avoid any suggestion of passion. When Siegfried is lying alone under the tree amid the mysterious murmurings of the forest the melody that accompanies his awakening thoughts of his mother:

should reach us 'as though from a distance'. But that effect will be created only if the crescendos are merely hinted at and their expression impersonal. The semiquaver triplet in the birdsong:

must be highlighted by accentuation; the clarinet must play it with the utmost tenderness. The prevailing mood of the scene is a deep calm, the stillness of high noon on a summer day, the sense of man and nature at one conveyed in the Greek expression: 'Pan is sleeping.' The phrase expressing Siegfried's annoyance at not being able to imitate the birds should be hurried and angry:

During the lovely clarinet melody, full of warmth yet very calm:

Siegfried should lean back against the tree-trunk in sensuous enjoyment, then take up his horn to blow his merry forest tune. Its performance must be exactly according to Wagner's directions. Above all it must not be hurried. For the first bars:

he gave the absolutely definite instruction: 'not fast and above all establish the theme'. Siegfried's heroic motive:

must be soft at first and very delicate; for all its expressiveness the delivery should not be emotional. He insisted that there should be no perceptible breaks between the repeated notes of the passage:

and that each should die away with a slight vibrato (*Erbeben*). He insisted that the whole of the following scene, the fight between Siegfried and Fafner, should take place in the background. The powerfully structured symphonic depiction of the fight, notwithstanding all the excitement, should not be over-emotional—a direction not hard to follow considering that, despite all the horrifying elements in the composition, Wagner avoided anything really excessive. The Siegfried theme when it is delivered just before the words, 'Viel weiss ich noch nicht':

should be slightly less animated. The performance of the dying Fafner's deeply moving speech was worked over with exceptional care. After the passage, 'Fafner, den letzten Riesen fällte ein rosiger Held', there must be a perceptible decrease in volume. As Wagner said, the many pauses in the speech express the dragon's growing weakness and this must be reflected in the quality of the singer's tone: his voice must sound more and more broken. Siegfried's response:

must be made without any hesitation and in a conversational, unsentimental tone of voice. The tempo should quicken somewhat as the birdsong re-enters on the flute:

and then, as Siegfried, having tasted the dragon's blood, puts his questions, 'Nützte mir das des Blutes Genuss? Das selt'ne Vög'lein hier, horch! Was singt es mir?', it should revert to a slower speed.

For if the tempo of the birdsong is taken too fast it is quite impossible to perform the difficult task of clearly articulating every word.

## Scene 3

At the stage rehearsals Wagner had nothing particular to say about the extraordinary dialogue between Alberich and Mime. The players had mastered their roles so completely that they provided a model for all future performances. Actually it is not easy to go wrong because the accentuation, correctly performed, will automatically produce the required interpenetration of musical and verbal stress. It is particularly difficult, however, to express strongly passionate yet furtively whispered lines with the greatest possible clarity of tone and speech. While Alberich is dominated by savage greed and a scornful sense of superiority, Mime is in a state of agitated confusion which finally becomes impotent fury.

Nor did Wagner feel any need to supplement the prescriptions of the score in the scene between Siegfried and Mime. At Siegfried's question, 'Im Schlafe willst du mich morden?', he warned against being misled by the expressive vocal line into making a ritardando. The significantly symbolic Curse theme after Siegfried's words, 'Neides Zoll zahlt Nothung, dazu durft' ich ihn schmieden':

must be played firmly, but without dragging. In the combination of three motives (the Work motive, the Horn-call and the Curse theme) during Siegfried's speech: 'In der Höhle lieg' auf dem Hort . . .' the accentuation of each phrase should be sharply defined, without any suggestion of urgency. The heavily weighted Giants' motive:

should be taken somewhat slower. From the third bar of the passage that starts with the delivery of a C major triad:

the tempo should become faster and the expression in every way lighter. Even the expressive cello melody must not occasion any rallentando. Wagner insisted that the heroic theme at Siegfried's 'Werd' ich das Feuer durchbrechen? Kann ich erwecken die Braut?':

should press steadily forward in strict tempo without being tempted by the significance of the motive to linger.

## Act III
## Scene 1

Wagner said of the powerful orchestral piece opening the third act that here we have 'Wotan's last ride, which is yet another descent to the underworld'. The performance must combine the utmost weight of volume and emphasis with an almost vocal eloquence. This applies especially to the bass melody:

The expression-mark 'animated, yet weighty' means that the dotted crotchet should be very heavily and the quaver very sharply accented. The overlapping entries of the Treaty motive must be brought out with the utmost precision;

likewise the entry of every new theme – the heavy chords of the striding Wanderer theme and all other symbolically significant motives.

But, when the Wanderer starts delivering his summons to Erda, the
volume and forte accents of the orchestra must be substantially
reduced. This must not lead to any slackness: the characteristic
profile of each motive should be no less sharply etched. When Erda is
singing, the accompaniment should always convey a sense of mystery
and gloom. At the words, 'Männerthaten umdämmern den Muth
mir', Wagner was especially insistent that the clarinets' delivery of
the World Mastery Motive:

should be very soft. In Wagner the manifold interweaving of motives
of reminiscence or premonition should always be treated as subordinate to the events actually happening: this indeed is the
fundamental stylistic principle that alone makes possible an effective
interaction of drama and music. Such moments – calling for restraint, not ecstasy – are the test of whether or not the players have
the secret of that style in their blood. The principle applies not only
to passages of veiled and twilit emotion but to those of power and
grandeur; thus the deeply sad, tender reminiscence of Brünnhilde:

must sound 'absolutely ghostly'. The way Erda's terrible questioning
brings home to Wotan the contradictions of his behaviour was very
impressive:

Although he compels her with his magic ('she can only withdraw when he allows her to', Wagner said) she is his superior in that it is from her lips that he hears the inexorable voice of his conscience which nothing can silence. So the expression here must reach an extreme pitch of intensity demanding the utmost exertion. Under Wagner's direction the demand was completely met. The same applies to the dagger-thrust of Erda's hasty, stammered outburst, 'Du bist nicht, der du dich nennst! Was kamst du, *störrischer* Wilder, zu stören der Wala Schlaf?', in which the words '*störrischer* Wilder' must be highlighted by incisive accents:

stör - ri -scher Wil - der.

Wagner expressly demanded that the Redemption theme as it enters after Wotan's words, 'Was in des Zwiespalt's wildem Schmerze verzweifelnd eins ich beschloss, froh und freudig führe, frei ich nun aus':

should be taken 'slightly faster' than the preceding bars and that it should be 'very brought out (*sehr heraus*)', as he tersely put it. He once characterized the spiritual significance of this theme (whilst going through the work at the piano) by the statement: 'It must sound like the proclamation of a new religion.' That this sublime theme should not be taken slowly might initially seem a contradiction. But this is not the case. Taken a shade faster the effect of the sudden illumination by which Wotan himself is overwhelmed is all the more powerful. The prescribed piano on the first crotchet of the second bar must be scrupulously observed : it is precisely the unexpected reduction of volume at that point which makes possible a deliberate increase of emphasis as the phrase broadly unfolds. Subsequently the performance of the whole scene must be imbued by this revelation of spiritual renewal. Wagner had nothing further to add to the directions in the score. Fidelity to these, together with an accurate perception of the significance of the marvellously interwoven basic motives, above all the sense of a boundless flow of feeling, ensures an infallible rendering of the emotional experience represented, the fusion of a movingly tragic act of heroic resignation with an exalted sense of the joy of life.

## Scene 2

'Without any passion': this was Wagner's instruction for the performance of the scene between the Wanderer and Siegfried. Every trace of pathos must be eliminated. In this dialogue we have Richard Wagner demonstrating to perfection his art of naturalistic representation in drama as well as in music. But his realism is of a very special kind. Like Goethe's and Shakespeare's its basis is a hidden metaphysical background. Thereby he rises far above common reality; we perpetually inhabit the sphere of elevated style. This must be borne in mind during performance. Vitality of expression must go together with clearly defined characterization. The deep feelings voiced from time to time by the Wanderer must be touched by a tender kindly humour and in Siegfried's outbursts of boyish arrogance the nobility of an essentially heroic nature must never be lost sight of. Wagner wanted the kindly, humorous theme that accompanies the Wanderer's 'ein Vöglein schwatzt gar Manches' played with a very precise rhythm ('très mesuré') and at a perceptibly slower tempo:

A short pause, indicated by the caesura of the example, should be made on the quaver rest of the first bar. When the theme makes its frequent reappearances the tempo should be livelier and the rhythmic accents should lose their initial equal stress and be adjusted to reflect the character of the dialogue. Before Siegfried asks: 'Doch darunter fehlt dir eine Auge?' he must bend a little so that he is looking up at the Wanderer from below. The passage:

Ich seh' mein Sohn, wo du nichts weisst, da weisst du dir leicht zu hel-fen

must be sung very calmly 'without any accent'; similarly the orchestra's quiet delivery of the Valhalla theme:

must be very gently played. The Wanderer's reaction to Siegfried's outburst, 'Weich' von der Stelle! denn dorthin, ich weiss, führt es zur schlafenden Frau: so wies es mein Vöglein, das hier erst flüchtig entfloh', is a moment of great importance; he is revealing his true nature as lord of the world. In anger he gives the peremptory reply, 'Es floh dir zum Heil; den Herrn der Raben errieth es hier: weh' ihm, holen sie's ein!', accompanied by bold and commanding gestures. A striking example of Richard Wagner's wonderful gift for making the inflections of speech express conflicting emotions was his demonstration to Siegfried of the correct delivery of the words:

Mit zer-focht - ner Waf - fe floh mir der Fei - ge?

Wagner's speech expressed a naive, questioning astonishment: one could see how the meaningful, illuminating words already stood on the threshhold of musical form (the initiated will see at a glance how the sense of the words is conveyed by a rising fifth followed by a falling one chromatically raised a semitone higher). In the powerful symphonic fresco, which depicts Siegfried striding through the sea of flames encircling Brünnhilde's rock and transports us by the vividness of its imagery, it is not the brilliant tone-painting that should predominate, but – as the structure of the piece makes clear – the thematic material, which must be strongly emphasized throughout. This also applies to Siegfried's horn-call which Wagner suggested should be played with the mouth of the instrument turned upwards:

and to the heroic theme:

which should ring out in appropriately imposing tones.

## Scene 3

The famous passage for unison violins:

was played very calmly and with that inner certainty of phrasing which only genuine sensibility and rich experience can achieve. While Siegfried is gazing at the sleeping Brünnhilde, the extended melody of Wotan's farewell song:

should have the quality of a reminiscence and accordingly be played softly, even when it becomes more passionate:

## Act III Scene 3

After Siegfried's 'Komm' mein Schwert, scheide das Eisen!' the horns' triplet following the Sword motive:

should be played very calmly and rather slowly, so that it serves as a transition to the melody for two solo clarinets which, played with extreme tenderness, so movingly expresses the first stirrings of Siegfried's desire:

When, having cut through the breastplate, he sees Brünnhilde in soft woman's dress he recoils, shocked and astonished. The accompanying violin passage should have the effect of a sudden rushing storm:

Only after a number of repetitions did the players succeed in executing this passage with the dashing virtuosity and at the same time eloquent expressiveness that Wagner wanted. During the melody, here transformed into an expression of passion (it was first heard from Fricka in *Das Rheingold*)*:

Siegfried gesticulates excitedly. Before singing the words, 'Wem ruf' ich zum Heil, dass er mir helfe?', he draws away somewhat from Brünnhilde. He should not look at her as he cries, 'Wie weck' ich die Maid, dass sie das Auge mir öffne?' 'Siegfried is frightened by the

* At 'herrliche Wohnung, wonniger Hausrat'. (Trans.)

thought of all he is about to undergo', Wagner explained. The orchestral rendering of his radical change of heart requires deep understanding. An *al fresco* representation will not do: rather, the breadth and compelling momentum of the performance must be combined with a detailed elucidation of the smallest particles of the motivic structure. In the passage that follows Siegfried's words, sung in a single breath:

every player must take the same care that he must take. The melody, played with perfect calm:

must suggest that the image of the sleeping Valkyrie is piercing the depths of Siegfried's heart. The ensuing viola solo:

should be taken more slowly; on the other hand the violin figure following Siegfried's question: 'Wie end' ich die Furcht? Wie fass' ich Muth?':

should be fast and strongly accented. The Sword motive after the significant words, 'Dass ich selbst erwache, muss die Maid ich erwecken!' should be decisive rather than loud. The melody (here making its first appearance):

should be sung with the utmost tenderness. The strokes above the
E and B of 'zitternd' indicate that here Wagner wanted that gentle
vibrato – not to be confused with the bad habit of a tremolando –
whose importance in expressive singing he often spoke of.

When Brünnhilde, awakened by Siegfried's kiss, slowly rises to a
sitting position, ceremonially greeting the earth and the heavens,
Siegfried, overawed, draws back somewhat. Her excitement is expressed by a slight trembling of her fingers that corresponds with the
figure of the harps:

The mounting scale:

must not be hurried but delivered in one broad sweep; it leads to an
unprecedented pitch of ecstatic exuberance, involving the whole
orchestra:

As Wagner put it, 'it is as though Brünnhilde were saying to herself:
"Now you are given to the world again!"' In her first utterance,
solemn, grand and marked by an exceptional firmness, 'Heil dir
Sonne! Heil dir *Licht*!', the word 'Licht' must be emphasized. At the
conclusion of her speech: 'Zu End' ist nun mein Schlaf; erwacht,
seh' ich: Siegfried ist es, der mich erweckt!', Siegfried is deeply
moved and the expression on his face must show this. His display of
feeling serves as a transition to the exultant outburst:

which leads to the one and only duet in which love and heroism interpenetrate. While they sing, each contemplates the other in deep astonishment. Interpreting the significance of this, Wagner said: 'It is as though a prophecy were being fulfilled.' During the orchestral postlude they must maintain an imposing stance. This postlude is the climax of the scene, a monumental structure of symphonic forms, in which the Wälsungen theme:

and Siegfried's heroic theme evolved from it (here for the first time in a radiant C major, and ending on the tonic):

together with a new motive expressive, so one feels, of the joy of liberated nature:

are boldly combined in counterpoint. The tension that has been holding us as though under a spell relaxes when Brünnhilde commences her loving, joyful song:

The re-entries of this melody – the cellos' delivery while she sings in a tone of lyrical contemplation: 'Du warst mein Sinnen, mein Sorgen du':

110

and then the violins':

should be played in a manner which Wagner liked to convey by the direction: 'as though without any feeling'. The initiated will know that he wanted the expression lifted to that sphere of which Schiller wrote: 'Extinguished every trace of earthly need.' But the lines, 'O wüsstest du, Lust der Welt, wie ich dich je liebt', and those that follow, must be intimately tender; Wagner characterized them very clearly by the pronouncement: 'Brünnhilde here is speaking like a mother to her child.' At first her manner is mild and friendly: 'Du wonniges Kind, deine Mutter kehrt dir nicht wieder', but when she reaches the line:

Du selbst bin ich, wenn du mich Se - li - ge liebst.

her expression grows gradually more intense; at the word 'Selige' it overflows with feeling, and then in the succeeding 'Was du nicht weiss, weiss ich für dich' calms down again. Throughout Brünnhilde's deeply emotional explanatory speech, shot through with moments of spiritual illumination, there should be 'little action'. At two points Wagner gave specific directions: Brünnhilde must put her hand to her forehead at the words, 'weil ich nicht ihn dachte' and then clutch her heart at the antithetical 'und nur empfand'. The psychological turning-point of the scene, after Siegfried's comment, 'Wie Wunder tönt, was wonnig du singst, doch dunkel dünkt mich der Sinn', Wagner defined by the statement: 'Up to this point Siegfried and Brünnhilde have been carried away, as though in the realm of the gods; now they begin to face each other as two persons.' Brünnhilde is still 'sublimely innocent', but in Siegfried the blood of the Wälsungs is stirring; at the orchestral figure:

his passion awakens and this must manifest itself in his gestures.

In the same way the tone of Siegfried's utterances must alter: he no longer exudes a high-spirited freedom, for now he is under the compulsion of an unknown, irresistible force of nature. This is what he is experiencing when, at the orchestra's cadential figure:

he is seized by a sudden anguish. Brünnhilde, too, is beginning to feel this; it is as though during the short interlude before her reply, 'Dort seh' ich Grane . . .':

she were seeking a pretext for deterring him. The motive:

must be somewhat stressed, and the subsequent quietly joyful melody:

should revert immediately to the former piano. Brünnhilde appears not to understand Siegfried; sadly she looks back on her former life – 'thinks of her little household', as Wagner humorously put it. But when she again attempts to evade Siegfried's mounting passion, 'now she knows what she is dealing with', and at her words, 'ich bin ohne Schutz und Schirm, ohne Trutz ein trauriges Weib!', we feel that her resistance is broken. Siegfried must deliver his 'Noch bist du mir die träumende Maid' 'in the trembling voice of one who is suffering', and lean against a rock as though in need of support. A little later, the passage:

Sangst du ____ mir nicht, dein Wis - sen sei das Leuch - ten der Lie - be zu mir?

must increase in intensity at 'das Leuchten der Liebe'. Every stage direction must of course be scrupulously observed; a small supplement is the demand that Siegfried should draw back somewhat from Brünnhilde as he delivers his exhortation, 'Tauch' aus dem Dunkel und sieh': sonnenhell leuchter der Tag!' It is, as Wagner said, a 'terrible moment' when Brünnhilde, at the height of her agitation, cries back: 'Sonnenhell leuchtet der Tag meiner Schmach!' He recited the words himself with the intensity he always displayed at such moments, the intensity of a flash of lightning, thrilling the spectator to the marrow. The final word, 'Schmach' ('this is the main point', Wagner said), is the one to be emphasized. Brünnhilde is now overwhelmed by dread; while the bass clarinet delivers its recitative after her outcry, 'O Siegfried! Siegfried! Sieh' meine Angst!':

*P* zurückhalten        *p* rall.

she sinks to the ground, and bending forward rests her hands on her knees. It is then that she experiences a vision of her former life, ideally free and happy. The orchestral prelude that expresses this:

*pp* dolce

should be as pianissimo as possible and so transcendentally ideal that it should sound as though coming from another world. The tempo should not be slow; special care should be taken to give a calm statement of the lightly flowing yet not insignificant triplet figure.

When Brünnhilde takes up the same melody in E minor ('Ewig war ich, ewig bin ich...'), she gradually raises herself from the ground. The phrase:

so be - rüh - re mich nicht.

must be heavily accented. Very significant to my mind is Wagner's remark that, at the words: 'O Siegfried, leuchtender Spross! Liebe dich und lasse von mir, vernichte dein Eigen nicht!', Brünnhilde must ignore the real Siegfried standing before her: 'she has an ideal in her mind and sings as though she were addressing the whole world (*singt wie in die Welt hinaus*)'. Emotion must reach a pitch of terrifying violence at Siegfried's vibrant outcry, 'Dich lieb' ich, O liebtest mich du!' And then the flood of his passion carries Brünnhilde away. During her speech, 'Fasst dich mein Arm, umschling ich dich fest...', he should not actually embrace her, but give the impression of wanting to and yet being restrained by inner timidity. 'Here everything is symbolic', Wagner said. In the bar:

the quavers of the triplet on the fourth beat must be taken at the same tempo as that of the preceding retarded quaver. At the words, 'Wie mein Arm dich presst, entbrennst du mir nicht?' Brünnhilde now really seizes hold of Siegfried. At the beginning of their final, heroic hymn of praise the lovers should not be looking at each other: 'they are addressing the whole world'. Although the score gives minute directions for the performance of the horn theme:

the lovers should not be looking at each other:

it is not all that easy to fulfil the composer's intention. Only intuitive feeling – the conductor's as well as the singers' – can achieve the desired result. To find the right tempo one must understand the whole; above all one should consider the passage where Siegfried and Brünnhilde, one after the other, sing the same melody (he at 'Sie ist mir ewig...' and she at 'Er ist mir immer...'). The predominating element throughout should be the expression of a sublime joy. The effect should be that of a ·celebration of life – a celebration in the face of which death and destruction appear to have lost their power.

Josef Hoffmann, Vienna: designs for *Götterdämmerung*, 1876
Above: Act III, Wild forest and rocky valley
Below: Final scene, Valhalla burning

# Götterdämmerung

## Prelude

The performance of the Norns' scene was characterized by a sense of grand objectivity. Here, where personified types, not individuals, are being portrayed, the basic expressive element must be one of sublime calm. The calm may be disturbed in places, but nothing should ever disrupt the continuously developing flow of melody and harmony. In this scene – the counterpart to that of the Rhine-maidens in that here it is the 'dark side of nature' that is being revealed – the Fate motive, which is the tragic motto of *Götterdämmerung*, is often sounded:

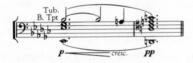

It should always be played with deliberately emphatic accents. The three Norns, who represent the three aspects of time – the past, the present and the future – should at first be absolutely motionless and their subsequent movements should be as limited as possible. Before they voice their secret runes they glance at the rope they are throwing to each other, as though they were reading off their knowledge from it. The crescendo of the softly sounded World Mastery motive:

117

should be very moderate, no more than a hint. When the second Norn hurriedly winds the rope round the crag, her tone of voice betrays her growing agitation: 'Des Steines Schärfe schnitt in das Seil . . .' The unison of their final utterance: 'Zu End' ewiges Wissen', conveys the premonition of tragic annihilation – one senses the approach of an inescapable destiny. The orchestra must depict the gradual daybreak with that purely intuitive phrasing which stylistically is so superior to the crudely naturalistic manner (still rife among the Italians). In the theme of the mature Siegfried evolved from the horn-call:

the two quavers of the third bar should be taken a trifle faster; the accelerando – which of course must not be exaggerated – has the effect of expressing the strength and confidence of Siegfried's intentions. When, after the fiery transition, the theme re-enters, fully armed as it were, with the Valkyrie motive serving as foil, it must be stated with its own peculiar might and grandeur. Every feature of its uncommonly rich rhythmic structure must be rendered with the utmost precision and with a feeling of strength held in reserve – as though the powerful tread of those ancient Germanic heroes who vanquished the legions of Rome were resounding once again. Siegfried and Brünnhilde's farewell scene must be animated throughout by an expression exultantly heroic and yet deeply passionate. Brünnhilde's face must light up with joy at Siegfried's jubilant 'Brünnhilde zu gewinnen': it should be as though she were exclaiming: 'How right you are!', Wagner declared. She should half embrace him as she utters her 'Gedenk' der Eide die uns einen', and then let him go as she delivers her admonitory 'Gedenk' der Liebe, die wir leben'. Since during the rehearsals Wagner seldom singled out anyone for special praise, it is worth mentioning that the extraordinary beauty of tone and expressiveness of the delivery of the passage:

Brünn - hil - de   brennt dann   e  -  wig   hei  -  lig   dir_____   in der Brust.

drew from him the involuntary exclamation: 'that was beautifully done!'\* When Brünnhilde puts Siegfried's ring on her finger, her singing of the words:

must convey a sense of rapture. At 'Nicht mehr schwingt es (Grane) sich muthig des Weges', when she laments she is no longer a Valkyrie, she distances herself from Siegfried. When in a tone of wonder she exclaims:

she leans back. The passage that follows her eloquently accented invocation to the gods (which the Greeks would have regarded as presumptuous):

namely, the passage: 'Getrennt – wer mag sie scheiden? Geschieden – trennt es sich nie', should be rendered with appropriate panto-mime. For all the radiant outpouring of their final exchanges, the passage should have the character of a leave-taking. For the performance of the symphonic episode depicting Siegfried's journey to the Rhine Wagner gave no special direction. His facial expression and characteristically eloquent gestures and hand movements were sufficient to spur the conductor to achieve the desired combination of plasticity, eloquent precision and perpetually forward-driving energy. But never must there be any suggestion of hurry.

## Act I
### Scene 1

We now enter a new world, pass from the boundless realms of na-ture into a settled, ordered society governed by strict laws of

---

\* 'Amalie Materna sang the role of Brünnhilde. (Trans.)

custom. This has a bearing upon both the performance of the music and the acting. The new motives:

and:

must be played with great precision and with a powerful tone even in the piano passages. The quavers of the latter theme should have a vigorous thrust, and, when they recur at Hagen's 'die beid' uns Brüder gebar':

additional weight. When Gunther angrily asks:

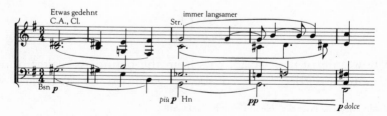

he rises from his seat and paces up and down the hall. As though by chance he approaches Hagen, who arrests his attention by a mysterious sign; at this moment the Magic Drink motive makes its first appearance, significantly preceded by a reminder of the Tarn-helm motive:

There is a touch of violence in Hagen's reply to Gunther's question: 'Was zwänge den frohen Mann für mich die Braut zu frei'n?':

Ihn zwän -ge bald dei -ne    Bit - te,

but he finishes the speech in the phlegmatic noncommittal tone that characterizes all his utterances. Only Hagen, who is always on the alert, hears a faint horn-call in the distance; he calmly begins his account of Siegfried's deeds giving no indication that he has heard. Gutrune meanwhile has filled the drinking-horn. The second horn-call, clearly defining Siegfried's motive, is heard by them all. Gunther springs from his seat. Shortly after the call has been repeated several times Hagen also rises. He moves to the back of the stage before he delivers his 'Hoiho! Wohin du heit'rer Held!' By now Gutrune too has risen. Siegfried's reply to Hagen's question:

Zu    Gi -bich's star - kem Soh - ne.

should be made very rapidly in strict tempo and with very incisive intonation.

## Scene 2

The motive:

refers to Gutrune; it expresses her look of involuntary longing. Through her stance and movements the singer should convey her feelings of astonishment and curiosity mingled with excitement. At this moment of suspense, Wagner wanted the stage to appear full of action: 'the more movement (motivated of course) the better', he remarked in passing. The rhythmic articulation of Siegfried's phrases could not be emphasized too strongly for him, especially the syncopations of:

Das biet' ich mit mir zum Pfand.

Siegfried's declaration of loyalty to Brünnhilde:

Ver - gäss' ich al - les, was du mir gabst, von ei - ner Leh - re lass' ich doch nicht

is not a lyrical outburst but an important psychological – ethical event; it must be sung without sentimentality and with the quaver triplets significantly emphasized. At 'Den ersten Trunk zu treuer Minne' Siegfried raises the drinking-horn. While the orchestra is playing the Magic Drink motive:

the expression on his face must indicate his loss of memory. 'Thinking and forgetting': Wagner's words give a clear idea of what he wanted. The syncopated E flat in Siegfried's violent outburst:

Ha, schön - stes Weib!

must be emphasized. In a voice trembling with emotion he puts the question:

Sind's gu - te Ru - nen, die ih-rem Aug'_____ ich ent ra - the?

and then with a sudden decisiveness continues: 'Deinem Bruder bot ich mich zum Mann: der Stolze schlug mich aus, trägst du wie er mir Übermuth, böt' ich mich dir zum Bund?' All this, especially the concluding:

böt' ich mich dir zum Bund

122

must be spoken with a violence that visibly frightens Gutrune, whose eye has been involuntarily meeting Hagen's. Regarding the transformation Siegfried has undergone, Wagner said it could be explained only if one assumes he has taken a poison which has thrown him, as though by magic, into a kind of fever whose first effects are enormously powerful. In the last line of Gunther's reply to Siegfried's semi-conscious questioning:

the name Brünnhilde must be accented and the voice die away as the phrase ends. The delivery of the Magic Drink motive before Gunther's 'Nie darf ich den Fels erklimmen, das Feuer verglimmt mir nie!':

must be very slow and drawn out: it should sound as though 'out of the void into the void'. The accompaniment of Hagen's preparations for the 'Blood-brothership' calls for a particularly vigorous performance; the sequence based on the Gutrune motive:

should have a powerful forward drive. Special attention must be paid to the moment when we have the feeling that Siegfried's sudden passion for Gutrune is a force of destiny impelling him. The high-spirited challenge of his 'Frisch auf die Fahrt!' must be very clearly conveyed by the orchestra's:

123

The first two beats must have an exceptional dash and freedom. The same applies to the repetition of this sequence later:

The swinging triplets must rush by, brimful of joy and good-humour. I well remember how Wagner conducted this piece when he presented it as a prelude to 'Hagen's Watch' at a concert in Vienna in 1875; one was completely carried away by that quality of his which the Italian term *incalzando* so aptly describes... During these events Hagen with phlegmatic calm is taking up his sword and shield. The bars that lead to his 'Hier sitz' ich zur Wacht, wahre den Hof' must be powerfully characterized. Wagner made a heavy rallentando on the first two beats:

and then reverted to a tant, propulsive rhythm for the horns' triplet. It goes without saying that nuances such as these must not be exaggerated and that they only come off when they stem from a deeply felt conviction. The postlude to Hagen's sinister song must be worked on with great care. The sculptured, deeply expressive quality of the motive is brought out to greatest effect by a declamatory style verging on speech. Above all, the melody that had accompanied the words, 'Ihr freien Söhne, frohe Gesellen' – that melody expressing an unrestainedly mocking scorn touched with a superior irony – must retain its character when repeated as a trumpet solo. The crescendo to a forte in the final statement of the uncannily transformed cry of the Rhinemaidens:

must be made with conscious deliberation.

## Scene 3

At the words, 'Ein Luftross jagt im Laufe daher', Brünnhilde rises from the rock upon which she has been sitting contemplating Siegfried's ring. When she hears Waltraute's call she moves to a rocky height at the back of the stage. As she puts her anxious question, 'O sag'! wär' wider mich Wotan's Sinn erweicht?', Waltraute makes a half-turn in a manner that bodes no good. During the three orchestral bars into which her passionately excited speech leads, Brünnhilde's gestures convey her rapture:

Waltraute's dark words throw her into a state of apprehension; as she exclaims: 'Was ist's mit den ewigen Göttern?', she reels back appalled. Wagner was insistent that the performance of Waltraute's great narrative should at no point be dragged. An epic style must be preserved; nevertheless, at every moment one must feel more or less acutely Waltraute's fear and feverish haste. This also applies to the recitative-like beginning:

125

At the end of the phrase:

die hat - te ein Held ihm ge - schla - gen.

a deliberate effect of pathos must be created by the drop of the voice on the lower note of the descriptive falling octave. At the passage:

sei - ner Ra - ben bei - de sandt' er auf Rei - se

the tempo must increase somewhat. Thereafter the atmosphere becomes increasingly charged with mystery; to an equal degree the expression of the voice and the orchestral motives must be one of muted significance:

The calm closing bars must be as pianissimo as possible. Up to this moment Waltraute has been almost motionless, her posture at times like that of a statue. But 'now', as Wagner put it, 'comes the action again' and it is impassioned and violent. Brünnhilde, who cannot understand Waltraute's anxiety, gently repulses her. As she asks: 'Mit blasser Wang', du bleiche Schwester? was willst du Bange von mir?', she lets drop the hand which she had been sympathetically holding. Her reply that she will never part with Siegfried's ring, 'Denn selig lacht mir aus ihm', is an impassioned declaration of love; but at the words:

it becomes a powerful rebuttal, reaching a pitch of exaltation at the passage, 'Geh' heim zu der Götter heiligem Rat', and above all at the expansively declaimed words:

Waltraute is beside herself and when, after her reproachful 'Dies deine Treue' Brunnhilde once again violently rejects her, she rushes away uttering piercing cries. All these fine shades of psychological – ethical feeling must be brought out by the stage action and tonal inflections of the singers.

The terrible overpowering of Brünnhilde by the Siegfried who appears in Gunther's form should be enacted with the utmost realism; any toning down would be wrong. After her shocked outcry, 'Verrath!', Brünnhilde moves swiftly down from the height she had mounted just before. Siegfried commences his speech:

in a disguised voice and an obviously uncertain tone. After the delivery – as though heartbroken – of the motive:

Brünnhilde raises herself a little at 'was könntest du wehren, machtloses Weib?' The prescriptions in the score regarding both the stage action and the music are so minutely detailed that it is impossible to misinterpret Wagner's intentions.

The passage:

was, according to his explicit instruction, altered to:*

## Act II
## Scene 1

The syncopated chords of the symphonic prelude:

should be absolutely piano after the initial forte entries; furthermore they should be adapted to the crescendos and decrescendos of the main melody in the bass so that full justice is done to its telling significance:

In the stage rehearsals Wagner let the whole dialogue between Alberich and Hagen pass without giving any further directions. In his report on the festival performances, he himself has described how perfectly the Alberich achieved the requisite whispered delivery, how his diction was a model of clarity, how, throughout, he conveyed the feeling of an uncanny daemonic presence. It is the

---

* The vocal score gives the unaltered version; the full score gives the altered notes in small print above the unaltered ones. (Trans.)

business of the conductor to ensure that the motives, which particularly in this scene hark back to previous events, are sharply defined and yet at the same time, in respect of both volume and accentuation, subordinated to the word and voice of the singer.

## Scene 2

The wonderful canonic piece, depicting nature's rebirth at the dawn of a new day, built on the bass clarinet melody and developed by eight horns:

was intoned and phrased with a delightful smoothness and captivating poetry. The conversation that ensues between Gutrune, Hagen and the returned Siegfried must be performed with the greatest possible ease and facility. 'A very detailed dialogue' – 'a kind of lively conversation on the stage to be kept wholly in the style of comic opera': these were the clues Wagner gave and only if they are strictly followed can the right effect be created: the feeling of exuberant joy expressed in Siegfried's coloratura-like effusions. In Gutrune's question:

the word 'Feuer' should be accented. Siegfried's reply, 'Ihn hätt' es auch nicht versehrt, doch ich durchschritt es für ihn' embarrasses her; as though smitten by a sudden shyness she draws back from him. When she is putting her jealous questions, Gutrune must be careful to preserve her individual tone of voice; she will succeed only if she has an instinctive feeling for the harmonic structure of her short melodic phrases. For the notation of melody linked to words presents only the surface of emotion; it is the harmony that reveals the underlying roots of thought and feeling. In the rhythmic melody:

Gutrune's voice should ring out with the joy she feels now that all her doubts have been dispelled.

## Scene 3

When one turns to consider the scene between Hagen and the vassals the term 'unprecedented' immediately comes to mind: here if anywhere it is applicable. It is as though the poet had conjured up from their graves the ancient Germans of Tacitus. The words and the music, charged as they are with defiant self-assertiveness, fearlessness and a strange, almost frightening humour, express the unique character of the German race. These heavy, striding phrases should be performed with a tremendous, ruthless energy and no trace of expressive pathos. Thus we have, even in moments of apparent gaiety, some apprehension of the tragic events to come. When the stierhorn is sounded:

the orchestra should slightly reduce its tone. Only at the 4/4 rhythm* should it swell out to a fortissimo again. The effect of Hagen's 'Hoiho!...' is thereby increased. The exchanges between the vassals, as they come hurrying on, and the sinister, imperturbable Hagen must be individually characterized. Music such as this could only have been conceived by the German imagination with its deepseated feeling for individuality. By infusing strongly accented speech with an incomparable variety of rhythms, a new, free contrapuntal style has been created. One must feel this in the performance... While the vassals deliver their greeting, Gunther stands calm and dignified; not until the uproar has ceased does he begin his speech. All eyes are turned upon Brünnhilde as she follows Gunther with downcast eyes and hesitating steps; Gunther

* When Gunther and Brünnhilde enter. (Trans.)

too is troubled. In his speech, 'Brünnhilde', das hehrste Weib...',
the line:

should be emphasized slightly, and the concluding 'Brünnhilde – und
Gunther, Gutrun' – und Siegfried' delivered with conscious pride.
At the sound of Siegfried's name, Brünnhilde raises her eyes,
horror-stricken, and Gunther involuntarily lets go of her hand.
While the vassals are muttering: 'Was ist ihr?', the two change their
positions. Every word of Brünnhilde's outcry, delivered as though
she were struggling for breath:

must be enunciated with the utmost vehemence. The vassals at this
point draw back somewhat from the principals. When Hagen comes
forward – previously he has been invisible – the dotted notes and
syncopations of the accompanying figure must be incisively
accented:

Brünnhilde draws closer to Siegfried before her pronouncement:
'Einen Ring sah ich an deiner Hand . . .'; after his calm reply, she
turns back to Gunther, who is thrown into confusion and struck
dumb by her question: 'Wo bargest du den Ring, den du von mir
erbeutest?' While the Tarnhelm motive is being sounded:

Brünnhilde's appearance is rigidly calm – then her fury breaks out and, in a loud voice for all to hear, she cries: 'Ha! – Dieser war's, der mir den Ring entriss: Siegfried der trugvolle Dieb!' Siegfried, absorbed in thoughts of the past, answers this terrible indictment as if in a dream:

Von kei - nem Weib kam mir der Reif, noch war's ein Weib, dem ich ihn ab - ge-wann!

Hagen is standing near to Brünnhilde as he asks: 'Brünnhild', kühne Frau! kennst du genau den Ring?' During her outburst, accompanied by grandiose gestures:

Heil' - ge Göt - ter, himm - li - sche Hü - ter

she comes right forward and asks:

Raun - tet ihr dies in eu - rem Rath?

in mysterious tones, as though speaking to herself. In the passage:

Schuf't ihr mir Schmach, wie nie sie ge - schmerzt,

the word 'Schmach' must be brought out. (In the score and in the piano transcription the penultimate bar of this example is rendered as:

The alteration was made by Wagner.) Brünnhilde is now as though lost to the world – a world to which her behaviour is completely unintelligible. After a fearful inner struggle with the uncontrollable forces taking possession of her, she cries out with clenched fists:

Ra - thet nun Ra - che, wie nie sie ge - ras't!

Gunther, raising his voice, endeavours to restrain her:

Brünn - hild'.    Ge - mah - lin!    Mäss' - - ge dich!

But she rebuffs him sharply and then, turning to the men and women around her, delivers the all-revealing, 'Wisset denn Alle: nicht – ihm – , dem Manne dort bin ich vermählt'. As she counters Siegfried's vigorous denial with her accusation, 'Du listiger Held, sieh' wie du lügst, wie auf dein Schwert du schlecht dich berufst', she must be standing close beside him. The final words of the ensuing passage:

Wohl kenn' ich sei - ne Schär - fe,    da - rin so won - nig ruht an der Wand    No -

- thung,    der treu - e Freund,    als die Trau - te sein Herr sich ge - wann.

in which she voices her seething emotions in tones of biting irony fused with unutterable tenderness, should be veiled: she is referring to a secret known only to Siegfried and herself. The vassals stride up to Siegfried pointing to him as they cry: 'Reinige dich, bist du im Recht!' The woodwind's repeated triplets, resounding through Brünnhilde's oath, 'Helle Wehr! heilige Waffe!...', should throughout be played with attack but always with a sudden reduction of volume at the piano passages. Gunther has drawn as far aside as possible from these disturbing events. After Brünnhilde's 'denn brach' seine Eide er all', schwur Meineid jetzt dieser Mann!', there is a general uproar. While Siegfried is reassuring Gunther – 'Glaub', mehr zürnt's mich als dich, dass schlecht ich sie getäuscht' – Brünnhilde stands apart as though it were no affair of hers: 'she is dead to the world'. After watching Siegfried's jubilant departure with Gutrune she sinks into a state of brooding: she must convey this by bending forward a little and remaining in this position as she sings:

Wel - ches Un'- hold's List    liegt____ hier ver - ho - len?

But the passion of her wounded heart intensifies; at the thought of Siegfried she utters a cry of misery, a cry in which the sentiment of revenge becomes an outburst of uncontrollable power, a rebellion springing from the core of her personality against the rapturous love which had once impelled her to give herself to Siegfried. At the penultimate bars of the orchestra's:

she is struggling for breath. Everything she has undergone, all her thoughts and emotions are compressed into the question delivered in a voice of steel:

which here drew from Wagner – as though he himself were swept by its elemental power – the exclamation: 'This is the most terrible moment!' At the words, 'mit dem ich die Bande zerschnitt', Brünnhilde looks up. As Hagen approaches her with his muted 'Vertraue mir, betrogene Frau!', she rounds on him contemptuously:

When she sings: 'nie reicht er ihm fliehend den Rücken: an ihm d'rum spart' ich den Segen' above the orchestra's:

Wagner said: 'Here she softens, tender memories are awakened.'
Gunther has throughout remained on the left-hand side of the
stage away from the other two. He has sunk to a half-kneeling
position at the foot of a column; in kneeling, his crown should fall.
Hagen's murderous desires now emerge: moving aggressively
towards Gunther he declaims in tones of biting mockery:

His dismissal of Gunther's weak lamentation must be hard and
obdurate:

When the horrified Gunther puts his timorous questions Brünnhilde interrupts him, striding firmly forward and crying: 'Dich
verrieth er, und mich verriethet ihr Alle!...' But when Gunther
expresses his sympathy for Gutrune: 'Doch Gutrune, ach! der ich
ihn gönnte...', she is 'stricken by the thought of Gutrune's enticing
charms' and, starting up violently, vents her rage and spite:

135

In this passage the great demands made upon the singer reach their culmination. Only by straining her physical and mental faculties to the limit did the Brünnhilde eventually succeed in realizing Wagner's intention. The psychology at this point is exceedingly complex: she is swept by a craving for revenge and at the same time an almost devilish jubilation. She must reach the extreme of ecstasy. The rise of the voice from E flat to B flat at the word 'Zauber' must be made with a crescendo ringing with wild destructive joy: the effect will be positively blood-curdling. The orchestral accompaniment, with its characteristic canonic imitation of the Gutrune motive, must be rhythmically precise but not too loud; in the last phrase, where the first violins are in unison with the voice, Wagner asked the players to put their backs into the task of supporting the singer's voice and her expression. The decision to destroy Siegfried having been agreed by all three, the force of expression sweeps to a climax of tense, propulsive rhythm, rigidly phrased. The close of the act with its sudden yet inseparable contradictions – the fearful threat of destruction and the overflowing *joie de vivre* – is unparalleled.

## Act III
## Prelude and Scene 1

The triplets of Siegfried's horn-calls blown on stage:

should be played brightly, the tempo continually pressing onward; the new Rhinemaidens theme likewise should not be dragged:

When the woodwind take over the main Rhinemaidens theme the figuration of the strings must be accordingly subordinated. The Rhinemaidens sang their trio with an enchanting tone-quality and gracefulness that greatly pleased Wagner. As their motive dies away:

Siegfried steps slowly downwards, lost in thought. He delivers the lines, 'Wie leid' ich doch das karge Lob?...' while he is descending. Flosshilde begins her reply to his call, 'He, he! ihr munt'ren Wasserminnen, kommt rasch: ich schenk' euch den Ring!', in a tone of somewhat mocking irony but with a deeply serious expression on her face:

The Rhinegold motive in the latter bars should be played very softly; here it should serve only as a gentle warning. As he delivers his calm challenge, 'So singet, was ihr wisst', Siegfried moves slowly forward. The Rhinemaidens' thrice-repeated call, 'Siegfried!' must be sung forcefully, each time accented with increasing intensity. The sequences built out of the World Mastery motive*:

should be played expressively, but the level of tone must be kept very moderate – only then does the mysteriously complex web of sound make its proper effect. At the lines, 'Traut' ich kaum eurem Schmeicheln, euer Drohen schreckt mich noch minder', Siegfried, who has remained standing half-way up the slope, calmly steps further down paying little attention to the Rhinemaidens. His 'Mein Schwert zerschwang einen Speer', accompanied by a fragment of the Treaty motive, and the ensuing lines:

* Accompanying their warning: 'Zu deinem Unheil wahr'st du den Ring.' (Trans.)

must be sung vigorously, conveying in his stance and by his gestures a defiant fearlessness. In the penultimate bar of the important passage:

the word 'Fluch' must be emphasized and the final words delivered with dismissive irony. After his outburst 'Leben und Leib' he throws his shield and spear to the ground. In order to secure absolute clarity of the words and notes the Rhinemaidens' difficult canonic imitations must not be hurried:

Throughout this final song they must give the impression of talking amongst themselves.

## Scene 2

At the orchestral figure:

# Act III Scene 2

Hagen steps slowly to the top of the slope. The triplet figure that accompanies the clarinet's melody*:

should flow quietly. The vassals, following Hagen, come down rather fast. The Gibichung theme at Hagen's speech, 'Der uns das Wild verscheuchte...':

should be played with characteristic terseness and rhythmic precision. While Siegfried is recounting his adventure with the Rhinemaidens all make themselves comfortable; the vassals settle themselves in a group around him and Gunther. The action should 'create the impression of a tumult that has gradually died down'. Siegfried should deliver the final words of his story:

with significant emphasis and a very serious expression. All are greatly disturbed and express this in their movements; some of the vassals stand up. To a melodic phrase appearing here for the first time, a phrase tinged with melancholy:

* After Siegfried's 'Kommt herab!' (Trans.)

one of the vassals hands Siegfried the drinking-horn he asks for. At the passage:

Siegfried's vivacity causes us to feel all the more strongly the harsh contrast between his unsuspecting high spirits and his impending doom. It is at a moment such as this that Richard Wagner displays the gift he shares with Shakespeare and Goethe of presenting the tragic with a frightening objectivity bearing no trace of sentimentality. At the line: 'Verstünd' er sie so gut, wie du der Vögel Sang!', Hagen leans towards Siegfried. The new motive:

should be taken at a comfortably heavy tempo (*sehr schwerfällig-behäbigen Tempo*), still somewhat slower than Mime's Work motive in *Das Rheingold*, but livening up with Hagen's reply, 'Die hoer' ich gern'. The Mime motive slows down again as Siegfried launches into the story of his early life, 'Mime hiess ein mürrischer Zwerg...':

Until Hagen administers his antidote reviving the memory of Brünnhilde the narration should be delivered calmly and equably in a strictly epic style. The accompaniment of only the string orchestra and horn (as organ-point) in the passage, 'auf den Ästen sass es und sang', recalling the song of the forest bird, should have transcendent tone-quality: it should sound 'as though from another world'. As he becomes more and more carried away by his story, Siegfried gradually rises from his seat on the ground; at the line, 'Wie mich brünstig umschlang der schönen Brünnhilde Arm!' he stands upright lost in rapture. When Hagen strikes him down, the vassals are paralysed with horror; then they rush up to Siegfried and lift him to a sitting position. The Fate motive, sounded just before Gunther's shocked 'Hagen, was thatest du?':

must not be played slowly. The unison passage:

requires especial attention. By making a powerful crescendo and by slightly altering the time-values of the rests to make them uneven, thereby bringing them alive, Wagner gave those two bars a quite extraordinary significance when he conducted the funeral music at the above-mentioned concert in Vienna (in 1875). It was like a revolt of the individual against the crushing weight of an overwhelmingly destructive tragic anguish. Regarding the performance of the funeral music – that unique heroic lament in the style of the ancient epics – Wagner gave no further directions. To a creation such as this, those words of Goethe, 'If you do not feel it, never will you find it', are more than usually relevant.

## Scene 3

To her own motive, which enters like a breath of fresh air and then becomes the expression of apprehension:

141

Gutrune steps rapidly into the hall. Before the line, 'Lachen Brünnhilde's weckte mich auf', she points to Brünnhilde's chamber. At
the bars:

she moves nearer to the door and stands lost in thought. The
fermata:

after she calls: 'Brünnhild', bist du wach?' must be lengthened so
that the effect of the silence is uncanny. The last word of the
sentence, 'So war es sie, die ich zum Rheine schreiten sah?' should
be somewhat stressed. Her motive just before Hagen's voice is heard
should be sounded very softly:

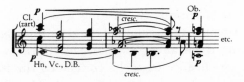

Now Hagen's voice is heard outside. His utterances should all be
rough and off-hand as though he were talking of unimportant
matters. At 'Der starke Held, er kehret heim', women hurry in
bearing torches. The last word of Gutrune's cry of horror, 'Was
bringen die?', must ring out sharply accented and then be abruptly
cut off. The horrified women rush forward. Before he answers
Gutrune: 'Siegfried, deinen todten Mann!', Hagen strides brazenly
to the middle of the stage. Wagner described the whole terrible
proceedings by saying 'Here we have, instead of a funeral procession, a procession of horrors (*Schreckenszug*).' When Gutrune faints
and Gunther is tending her, he clasps her hands at the words,
'Gutrune, holde Schwester...'; as she recovers she pushes him
violently away. Stepping defiantly forward, Hagen addresses his
words, 'Ja denn, ich hab' ihn erschlagen...', to the whole gathering,

but he does so with face averted and a furtive expression. The brothers' struggle for the ring – 'the giants' struggle in *Das Rheingold* is repeating itself', Wagner remarked – and Gunther's death quickly follow. When Hagen is on the point of drawing the ring from Siegfried's finger to the searing delivery of the World Mastery motive:

and the corpse threateningly raises its hand to the Sword motive, the women standing by utter a shriek of horror. Brünnhilde has heard this shriek, the culminating expression of all the horrors that have been heaped upon us. The 'Significantly slower' tempo direction must not be exaggerated; the tempo should be treated as a broad andante alla breve, typical of the older Church music and employed by Beethoven in the Kyrie of the *Missa Solemnis*. As Brünnhilde ceremonially strides forward, Hagen picks up his shield from the ground. The scene has the grandeur of antique tragedy; Brünnhilde resembles, as Wagner put it, 'an ancient German prophetess'. All human passions extinguished, she is now a pure eye of knowledge – and the spirit of love that has taken possession of her, a world-conquering, redeeming love, carries her beyond all fear of death. There is no bitterness in her speech to Gutrune, 'Armsel'ge schweig', sein Ehrgemahl warst du nie...' 'She regards her as a poor deceived creature.' In Gutrune's desperate outburst, 'Verfluchter Hagen...', the words, 'Wie jäh nun *weiss ich's*' must be especially emphasized. She bends over Gunther's corpse as though she were dying; the last bars of the passage:

signify the moment of her death, Wagner said. Her fate has been fulfilled. After the twice-repeated Fate motive:

# Götterdämmerung

Brünnhilde takes her decision; her gesture expressing this must exactly coincide with the incisively rhythmic orchestral figure:

As she delivers her words of command, 'Vollbringt Brünnhilde's Wort', she turns one way and then the other with sweeping arm movements. Her majestic bearing impresses upon everyone the justness of her cause. When she sees Siegfried in her mind's eye, the ideal hero radiant in all his glory, she is lost to her surroundings: 'she is not speaking to the people, it is like a wonderful vision'. The Sword motive at the passage, 'schied er sich durch sein Schwert' should not be too loud. The exclamation:

Ver-fluch - ter Reif!

must be forceful and cutting. The World Mastery motive:

and the ensuing Curse motive must be as pianissimo as possible. Brünnhilde is now inspired as never before; she is swept by a sublime joy reducing all worldly cares to nothing. For all their heartfelt warmth, the bars:

144

should be delivered with great calm by both singer and orchestra. The performance of the symphonic conclusion, 'saying everything', of this cosmic drama, in which the spirit of antique tragedy and that of Shakespeare seem to have joined hands, demands of the conductor a grip of iron; like a Cyclopean wall the themes and melodies must pile themselves up before us.